WHICH FORK DO I USE WITH MY BOURBON?

WHICH FORK DO I USE WITH MY BOURBON?

Setting the Table for Tastings, Food Pairings, Dinners, and Cocktail Parties

Peggy Noe Stevens & Susan Reigler

FOREWORD BY FRED MINNICK

south limestone

Published by South Limestone Books
An imprint of the University Press of Kentucky

Editorial and Sales Offices: The University Press of Kentucky
663 South Limestone Street, Lexington, Kentucky 40508-4008
www.kentuckypress.com

Library of Congress Cataloging-in-Publication Data

Names: Stevens, Peggy Noe, author. | Reigler, Susan, author.
Title: Which fork do I use with my bourbon? : setting the table for
    tastings, food pairings, dinners, and cocktail parties / Peggy Noe
    Stevens and Susan Reigler ; foreword by Fred Minnick.
Description: Lexington : South Limestone, 2020. | Includes
    bibliographical references and index.
Identifiers: LCCN 2019046944 | ISBN 9781949669091 (hardcover) | ISBN
    9781949669107 (pdf) | ISBN 9781949669114 (epub)
Subjects: LCSH: Cooking (Bourbon whiskey) | Bourbon whiskey. |
    Cooking—Kentucky. | LCGFT: Cookbooks.
Classification: LCC TX726 .S74 2020 | DDC 641.2/52—dc23
LC record available at https://lccn.loc.gov/2019046944

Manufactured in the United States of America.

To the Kentucky bourbon industry,
which made it possible for us to have careers
drinking bourbon. Cheers!

CONTENTS

FOREWORD

When my buddy called and said, "Let's have a bourbon tasting," I said, "Absolutely" and pulled about fifteen bourbons to take to his house. I showed up with the whiskeys, and we poured them and sipped. Then we just looked at each other and said, "Now what?"

We ordered Chinese food and watched football. It was as if I were back in college, frat-boying it up—only I was an adult. I went to fancy restaurants now rather than eating at Taco Bell, and I wore nice clothes instead of frayed jeans and faded T-shirts. At the time, neither of us would admit it, but other than enjoying the good bourbon, we were bored. Sadly, this wasn't my only boring tasting. Many others have been dismal failures on the fun meter. We tasted. And that was it.

From what I've observed over the past fifteen years, that's the story among many whiskey drinkers. Many of us don't know how to entertain. Oh, sure, we can drink and shoot the breeze, but our hodgepodge of glasses and limited snacks (Kraft American cheese slices and apples, in my case) consistently prove that our only focus is the bourbon. Well, thank goodness my good friends Peggy Noe Stevens and Susan Reigler decided to write *Which Fork Do I Use with My Bourbon?* to take the guesswork out of entertaining for us less sophisticated types.

After reading this great work, I'm now wondering about all my tastings that have gone astray. What if I had served proper food to accompany what we were tasting and even had décor to match? What if I had coordinated what we were tasting, pitting wheated bourbons against ryes, instead of just randomly grabbing bourbon off the shelf? I've often pondered how successful I've been at showing my friends the true hospitality of bourbon. And now I know. I've been awful. There is a bright side, though: after reading this book, I know how to entertain.

Which Fork Do I Use with My Bourbon? will answer questions such as when to have a buffet and when to have a sit-down meal, including table settings and where to seat people. But it will also help you remember the little things, like supplying a small ice bucket with tongs. How many parties have you been to where you've had to scoop ice with a plastic cup or use your hands?

Stevens and Reigler weave their massive bourbon knowledge into their brilliant how-to approach. Even if you're a whiskey geek, you'll find the information helpful and the suggestions doable. For instance, don't place fragrant flowers near your bourbon tasting. Who wants to smell roses when you're trying to nose the delicate aromas of Basil Hayden? The authors provide never-before-published food-pairing tips that prove to the world that bourbon can be just as flexible as wine at the dinner table. But more than anything, Reigler and Stevens are true experts in their respective fields. At a time when everybody claims to be an authority and anybody can start a blog, you really have to vet the information you obtain from mainstream news sources, and sadly, this has crossed over into bourbon facts as well. But Reigler was writing about bourbon in the 1990s, long before it was cool, and Stevens was the first female master taster. So if they tell me to fold my napkin a certain way and not to seat Uncle Bob next to Aunt Caroline, I'm going to listen. And if the woman who created the first pairing wheel advises me to drink a high-proof bourbon with my salad, by god, I'm going to do it. The authors have not come up with these recommendations on a whim. Every idea has been thoughtfully considered, tested multiple times, and comes with the full support of an industry that hangs on every word these women write.

This book will change how you throw parties, and it will help you find your own entertainment style. And most important, in your circle of friends, you'll be the cool one because you know which fork to use with your bourbon.

FRED MINNICK

INTRODUCTION
Kentucky Bourbon Style

Kentuckians have been entertaining, with bourbon in hand, for more than 200 years. Over the decades, early frontier gatherings evolved into some of our favorite ways to entertain. Tailgating at college football games and reveling in the infield at Churchill Downs on Derby Day are direct descendants of "dinner on the ground." Barn dinners were once as commonplace as summer meals in tented pavilions today. The feast spread out on the sideboard for hunters after the morning shoot has become brunch.

As is the case with any regional cuisine, Kentucky's food and drink are tied to a combination of nature and culture. Corn grows extremely well in the Ohio Valley, so when settlers arrived in Kentucky in the late eighteenth and early nineteenth centuries and started farming, corn was a major crop. Distilling was a common farm activity, not only to make whiskey (and fruit brandies) for personal consumption but also to utilize surplus grain. The farmers who brought their stills with them from New York and Pennsylvania had been distilling rye whiskey, but in Kentucky they had corn. Eventually, that corn-based whiskey became what we know today as bourbon.

Of course, corn was also eaten: roasted corn, corn on the cob, corn pudding, grits, and corn bread were just a few common Kentucky dishes. Cornmeal was used as breading on such delicacies as fried green tomatoes and fried oysters (oysters were shipped up the Mississippi and Ohio Rivers from New Orleans). To this day, fried oysters and grits are found on the menu in many Kentucky restaurants.

Sugar was an expensive commodity on the frontier, but a crop called sorghum grew plentifully. Crushing its stems and boiling the sap yielded a syrup that was a flavorful substitute for molasses.

Game was plentiful in Kentucky, and vegetables grew easily. One traditional dish was burgoo stew, using whatever game or domestic meat (chicken, pork, beef, or lamb) was available and seasonal vegetables (see chapter 7). Aged, salt-cured hams—today called country hams—were an important Kentucky product. Kentucky is still part of the "country ham belt," which includes Virginia, Tennessee, and Missouri.

A traditional way to serve country ham, especially as a party food, is on beaten biscuits, another regional specialty. Making them requires a special machine that stretches and compresses the dough (the old ones were cranked by hand). Beaten biscuits differ from ordinary biscuits in that they are small (about the size of a half dollar) and dense, almost hard. To pry them apart to add sliced ham, they have to be warmed in the oven for a few minutes. They are well worth the trouble.

Another Kentucky delicacy worth mentioning is Henry Bain's sauce. Henry Bain was the headwaiter at Louisville's private Pendennis Club in the early twentieth century. He came up with his own version of steak sauce that has a distinctive flavor thanks to the use of pickled walnuts in the recipe. Once you've tasted it, you'll never go back to using A-1. Much more than just a steak sauce, it also crops up as a condiment in other contexts, such as topping a block of cream cheese that is sliced and served on crackers.

Kentuckians even have a special (and favorite) salad ingredient: Kentucky Bibb lettuce (sometimes called limestone Bibb). John Bibb was a nineteenth-century Kentucky state legislator and an amateur horticulturist. In 1865, in his Frankfort garden, he developed the tender-leaved, buttery lettuce variety that bears his name.

Perhaps more than any other food or drink, bourbon is associated with Kentucky, and two centuries of history have made the product what it is today. Over the years, Kentuckians have distilled corn and shared the result—bourbon—with family and friends. In days gone by, truly special guests in a Kentucky home would be served the "family whiskey"—that is, the best whiskey, which was usually reserved for family members. In short, Kentuckians have always known how to have a good time, with a flourish, and we've written this book so that you can too.

Our Goals

Most of all, we wanted to share our Kentucky family secrets related to entertaining and our insights into everything bourbon. When we travel all over to conduct bourbon tastings, we are constantly asked, "How do I do this in my home?" So we decided to share our knowledge and experience in this book to help bourbon lovers who want to entertain. Rather than a run-of-the-mill cookbook, it is more of a how-to guide to bourbon entertaining. Of course, we also include a few of our favorite recipes and some recipes from various distilleries that showcase how they do things. Like good Kentucky hosts, we want to share our "family whiskey" with you.

It is truly your own style that matters, and we hope our suggestions will help you discover that style and hone it along the way. Not all parties require you to work your fingers to the bone planning and executing. The best form of bourbon etiquette is simply to make people feel comfortable. Whiskey making is about quality and authenticity. Likewise, authenticity plays a big role in your personal entertaining: the best gift you can give to your guests is yourself. Entertaining should be a reflection of your personality, the way you live, the interaction of friends and family—your lifestyle.

A Disclaimer

Neither of us is employed by any distillery. We value all Kentucky bourbon producers and have included a variety of bourbons in the recipes in this book. Which bourbon you choose to use in the cocktails and dishes depends on your own individual taste. Once you've tasted a few, you will know what you like.

Also, in some of the recipes we name ingredients from specific companies. We have received no remuneration to mention or endorse these products. We simply think they are excellent.

ONE

Planning the Perfect Party

Keeping one's guests supplied with liquor is the First Law of Hospitality.
—*Margaret Way*

WE'VE ALL ATTENDED PARTIES where the host looks exhausted and seems eager for the guests to depart. Why does that happen? It's a party, and it's supposed to be fun! All too often, last-minute arrangements or simply a lack of planning can create a hectic and unorganized atmosphere, which is certainly no way to celebrate what should be a happy occasion. The best gift you can give your guests is to enjoy your time with them. It's up to you to set the tone, but being in the moment at your own party can be difficult as you try to keep track of all the details. The seemingly endless tasks of serving the food, refreshing the cocktails, and answering the door as new guests arrive can be overwhelming. That's why thinking ahead is vital.

Any successful fete that both the guests and the hosts enjoy must be well executed. Organizing countless celebrations, conferences, galas, and home parties has taught us all the tricks when it comes to planning. Let's begin with three basics:

- Give your party a purpose. What is the occasion? This may sound simple, but it helps to establish a theme for the event and to decide whether the party will be informal or formal.
- Don't leave your guests guessing. Send the invitations well in advance: two to four weeks for informal events, and four to six weeks for more formal affairs. The design and look of the invitation should indicate what type of event your guests will be attending. Save-the-date notifications are helpful in advance of the actual invitation if it is a busy time of year, such as the holidays. That way, people can mark their calendars. Regardless of the type of invitation (see the samples provided)—and whether informal or formal—it should always answer the who, what, when (both start and end times), where, and dress code. "RSVP" (in French, répondez s'il vous plaît) requests a response from everyone, whether they plan to attend or not; alternatively, you may ask guests to respond with "regrets only" to make things easier. Include directions for guests who have never been to your home. If you are inviting fewer than ten people, add a personal touch and give everyone a phone call.

- Create and update the guest list. Making the list can be easy enough, but hunting down email and physical addresses can be tedious. Use the same list to mark down RSVPs; it is essential to have an accurate head count so you can purchase the right quantities of food and beverages. There are some great online invitations that will automatically keep track of your guests' responses.

The General Plan

The time of day, the season, and the nature of the party will help you decide what food and cocktails to serve. Hearty hors d'oeuvres or buffet? Sit-down dinner or light reception? Think about who your guests are

Guest List

Name _____

Address _____

_____

Phone _____

R.S.V.P. ☐ Number in Party _____

Name _____

Address _____

_____

Phone _____

R.S.V.P. ☐ Number in Party _____

Name _____

Address _____

_____

Phone _____

R.S.V.P. ☐ Number in Party _____

Name _____

Address _____

_____

Phone _____

R.S.V.P. ☐ Number in Party _____

Name _____

Address _____

_____

Phone _____

R.S.V.P. ☐ Number in Party _____

Name _____

Address _____

_____

Phone _____

R.S.V.P. ☐ Number in Party _____

Name _____

Address _____

_____

Phone _____

R.S.V.P. ☐ Number in Party _____

Name _____

Address _____

_____

Phone _____

R.S.V.P. ☐ Number in Party _____

Please join us for a

COCKTAIL PARTY

The Stevens Home
1 Bourbon Lane
Louisville KY, 12345

Saturday, June 1
5:00pm to 7:00pm

RSVP Peggy Noe Stevens
name@emailaddress.com
333-555-4444

Dress: Casual

A night of good friends and good cheer!

Cocktail Party Invitation
5 x 7

PARTY TRICK—Take a graphic from the invitation, such as a cocktail glass, and include it on signs for the buffet or bar and on place cards for the dining table. This carries your theme throughout the party.

PLEASE JOIN US FOR A

BOURBON & BITES

FOOD PAIRING PARTY

Enjoy a Unique Pairing of Bourbon Bacon, Chocolate & Cheese

Dress: Casual

The Stevens Home
1 Bourbon Lane
Louisville KY, 12345

Saturday, June 1
5:00pm to 7:00pm

RSVP Peggy Noe Stevens
name@emailaddress.com
333-555-4444

Bourbon & Food Pairing Invitation
5 x 7

BOURBON *Dinner*

You are cordially invited to a Bourbon Dinner
at the home of Peggy Noe Stevens

1 Bourbon Lane ~ Louisville KY, 12345
Saturday, June 1 ~ 6:00pm to 8:00pm

Enjoy a Five-Course Dinner Paired with
Michter's | Bulleit
Angel's Envy | Four Roses
Woodford Reserve

Dress: Semi-Formal

RSVP Peggy Noe Stevens | 333-555-4444

Bourbon Dinner Party Invitation
5 x 7

and what type of food they would enjoy, especially those with dietary restrictions. Keep track of this information in case you choose to duplicate the party next year.

The Floor Plan

Nothing is more personal than inviting people into your home. Do a mental walk-through, beginning with the arrival of your guests, to determine the location and flow of the various elements of the party. Ask yourself: Will you have any décor leading up to the entry? Once guests are inside, do you need to make arrangements to collect their coats? Are guest restrooms ready with candles, soap, towels?

Ideally, guests should have plenty of room to walk around. It is no surprise that the bar will probably be the star of the show and where guests will gather first. To prevent everyone from ending up in the kitchen, give each element of the party its own real estate, according to

PARTY TRICK—
If you are inviting a special guest that everyone will want to meet, or if the party is a celebration of someone's birthday, create a unique cocktail, punch, or dish and name it in honor of that special guest.

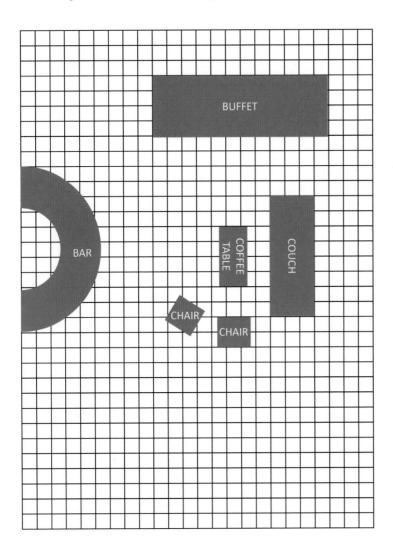

its function or importance. Here is a list of stations to consider:

- Parking area or valet
- Walkway
- Entrance
- Restrooms
- Coat check
- Host gift table
- Welcome bar or welcome cocktail
- Hors d'oeuvres station(s)
- Buffet
- Sit-down dinner
- Dessert station
- Departure gifts for guests (optional)
- Backup plan for outdoor events (in case of inclement weather)

The Décor

Décor is easy to collect once you have chosen a theme. You may be surprised by how many trays, vases, candleholders, and other accessories you already have on hand. Consult your list of bar and buffet or dinner stations to determine the size and quantity of props required. Creating a visual collage of the items allows you to see how well the theme is carried through. Consider color, height, shape, and texture, and pay attention to how everything looks together.

PARTY TRICK—Shop at vintage furniture stores for inexpensive, one-of-a-kind decorating accents.

Winter props vignette

Spring props vignette

PARTY TRICK—
Hester & Cook, a
paper goods company
in Nashville, Tennessee,
sells a wide variety
of table décor (place
mats, table runners,
napkins, name cards)
with seasonal themes.
The designs are stylish,
and the products are
a great value. Browse
its website at https://
hesterandcook.com.

Fall props vignette

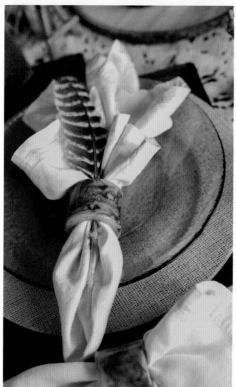

Following are lists of props with seasonal themes, but your party decorations can be based on any theme, holiday, or occasion. The goal is to collect and arrange your props in advance so that they mirror your theme.

Winter

Sprayed or natural branches
Glass napkin rings
Glass punch bowl
Silver-rimmed Manhattan glasses
Frosted plates
Tiered silver tray
Silver ice bucket
Silver flower vase

Spring

Pussy willow, forsythia, jonquil
Clear glass pitcher
Yellow tablecloth

Floral napkins
Ice-blue plates
Blue glass decanter
Glass ice bucket
Shell napkin rings
Simple syrup holders with bird finial

Summer

Copper ice bucket
Palm branches
Linen and jute table runner (white)
Cream serving pieces
Black candleholder with white candles
Slate tasting mats
Black rattan lanterns
Clear glass decanter
Small copper tasting glasses and rocks glasses

Fall

Cowhide runner
Tin platters
Wooden serving platter
Horn centerpiece and accents
Amber punch glasses and pitcher
Turkey feathers and pinecones
Wooden place-card easels
Wooden ice bucket

The Food

As always, think seasonally when it comes to the food for your party. And plan your food offerings to coincide with the length of the event. For example, if you will be serving hors d'oeuvres for three hours, you may want to provide several variations throughout the evening, or you can make large quantities that will last for the entire party. There are plenty of nonseasonal food choices as well, including bakery-fresh breads, artisanal cheeses, and nuts. Regardless of the selections, presentation is everything; it can actually make the food more enticing and should mirror your theme.

PARTY TRICK— Gather your recipes well ahead of time. Then make your grocery list by category—meats, vegetables, cheeses, condiments, crackers, and breads. This will save shopping time.

Layered presentation using feathers as a base and a wooden tray

Layered presentation using a metal tray and pistachio base to add visual interest and color

PARTY TRICK— To add background color and visual interest to hors d'oeuvres, line the trays or serving platters with materials that provide a pop of color or a seasonal tone. Some suggestions are banana leaves, beds of herbs, chopped nuts, or linen napkins.

PARTY TRICK—
Planning to cook?
Note the preparation
and cooking times
for each recipe so you
can devise a schedule
and avoid being
stuck in the kitchen,
leaving yourself
plenty of time to
get ready and then
socialize with your
guests.

Hors d'oeuvres and Appetizers

Passed hors d'oeuvres are ideal at a party so that guests can enjoy the food while keeping their conversations going, but you need extra hands to serve them. Alternatively, you can set up several stations with different hors d'oeuvres at each to keep everyone circulating. Whether hors d'oeuvres are passed or stationary, they should be bite-sized and easy to manage.

Appetizers served prior to a dinner or a buffet should be fairly light. You don't want everyone to fill up before dinner! Choose a selection of hot and cold items, since this offers guests a variety and helps free you from the kitchen. It is best to choose appetizers with diverse ingredients (not all cheese, for example), and you should balance the menu from savory to salty, earthy to sweet. Make sure the appetizers are ready to serve when the guests arrive. Check periodically, and replenish as needed.

The quantity of appetizers is always based on the length of the party, but if appetizers will precede a substantial meal, three choices are ideal. If there will be no meal, count on offering six to eight choices.

The Buffet

Assembling a buffet is always a matter of logistics, but if you think of the buffet as a landscape, it becomes quite easy (see the accompanying diagrams). Thinking about the actual courses and how people will physically proceed through them is helpful as well.

You have already chosen the appropriate props and platters, china, glassware, and silverware. Now you have to think about placement. The most interesting buffets are not only visually inviting but also delightfully surprising, especially when they deviate from the flat tabletop. Elevate a few items by securing a small wooden block or a stack of covered plates underneath the serving dishes. Two- and three-tier stands can also be used to add height, and they make great bread, hors d'oeuvres, and sweets trays.

If the number of guests will exceed twenty-five, you might consider a double-sided buffet, allowing diners to venture down both sides of the buffet table to avoid a long line. Note that the bread should always be the last food item on the buffet table. This ensures that the bread won't get soaked in the juices of the side dishes and entrée too early. Flatware and napkins are also last in line, so the guests don't have to fumble with the silverware while doing a balancing act with their plates. Napkins can reflect the formality or casualness of the party. Nice-quality three-ply paper napkins better absorb moisture on cocktail glasses and messy hors d'oeuvres. Use cloth or linen napkins for sit-down meals and buffets. The napkins for buffets can actually serve a dual purpose if you roll the silverware inside them.

PARTY TRICK—
Line up your favorite place mats to make a table runner. You can hide the seams with décor.

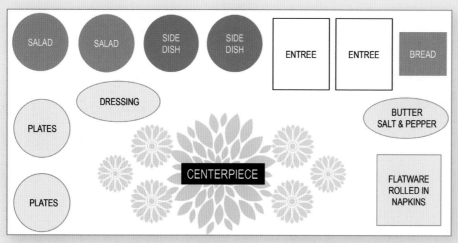

Single-Sided Buffet Diagram

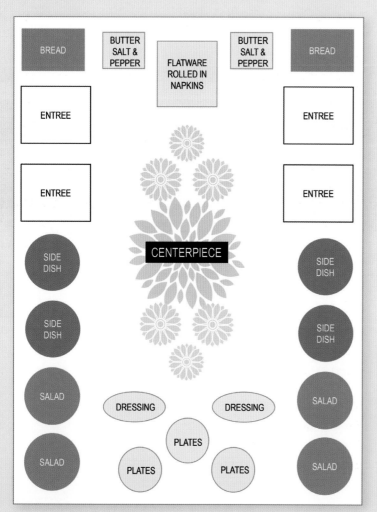

Double-Sided Buffet Diagram

PARTY TRICK—Write the name of each food item on a Post-it, stick it on the serving platter or tray you will be using, and then arrange the dishes on the table. This helps avoid last-minute placement decisions and ensures that there's adequate space. (Don't forget to remove the notes before guests arrive.)

The Sit-Down Dinner

Sit-down dinners should accommodate conversation, so keep center-pieces low to allow your guests to see one another. Sit-down meals can be as decorative and inviting as buffets, depending on the table setup. To add dimension, try a layered look for place mats, plates, and napkins. Think about texture and color as you design the theme. You'll notice that the table settings for our bourbon parties include no wineglasses. But we do appreciate a great cocktail and pairing with our meals. We always provide water glasses, as well as decorative glassware to hold bourbon.

Formal place setting incorporating the cocktail glass

Casual place setting

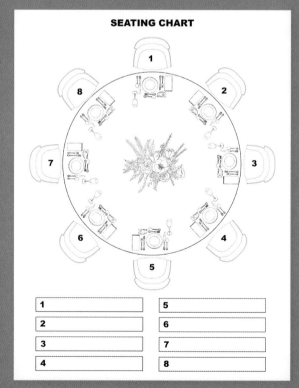

SEATING CHART

1		5	
2		6	
3		7	
4		8	

Gifts for Guests

If you like, you can create a small token of appreciation for guests and give each one a keepsake that mirrors the party's theme. For example, for a Derby theme, a four-piece box of bourbon candy and a miniature bottle of your favorite bourbon decoratively tied together would be ideal. From small potted mint plants to horseshoe coasters, such gifts express a generous thank you from the host. They are certainly optional but always appreciated.

Regardless of a party's style, theme, or décor, your guests will appreciate the thought put into your entertaining and those special little touches. A bit of planning goes a long way to ensure a memorable experience.

TWO

Setting Up the Perfect Bourbon Bar

GATHERING AROUND A BAR at a party is as natural as putting a block of ice in your bourbon. So why are party guests invariably drawn to the kitchen like magnets to the refrigerator door? The kitchen is exactly where the host doesn't want everyone to be, where they can see what goes on behind the curtain, so to speak.

Another common party scenario occurs in the proverbial "basement bar," where helpful cries of, "You're out of ice! We need more glasses! The bourbon's almost gone . . . got any more of the good stuff?" are all too common. Sweat on brow, the host races around washing glassware, filling the ice bucket, and simultaneously wrestling an exuberant guest away from the prized bottle of silent-auction bourbon.

It does *not* have to be this way. You can set up the perfect bourbon bar in your home so that you won't be run ragged and guests won't end up in the kitchen. All that's required is a simple lesson in real estate, traffic flow, and hospitality.

You might think that food reigns at a party, but does it really? Quite naturally, the first thing we offer a guest is something to drink, whether it's coffee or tea, a cocktail, or a glass of wine. The first question from the server after you are seated in a restaurant is about your choice of beverage. Think of the bar as your first welcome to guests. Everyone immediately looks for the bar after breezing into your house. The bar is the star of the show. No matter the size of your space, the cardinal rule of real estate applies to setting up the perfect bar: location, location, location.

First, imagine a "helicopter view" of your home. This gives you a good idea of how to best use the available space. Choose a bar location away from the appetizer table or buffet to avoid a traffic jam. Guests should be able to move through the house, creating flow and conversation, and the bar should be positioned for easy access.

People tend to swarm the bar like bees to honey, so allow ample space around it. If you already have a permanent bar in your home, that's easy enough. But if you're using a table, cover it with a cloth that touches the floor. The cloth can match the décor of your home or echo your party theme. It serves the double duty of looking nice and hiding ice and backup bottles stashed under the table.

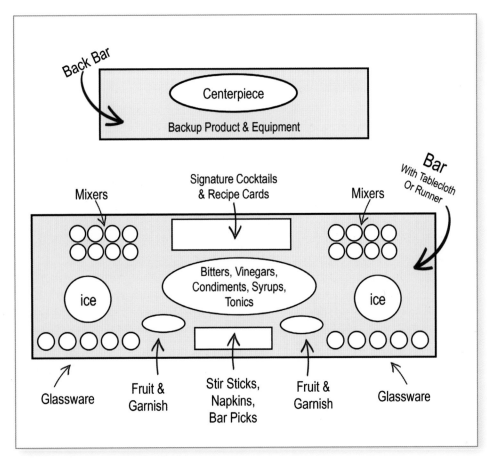

Back Bar

Centerpiece

Backup Product & Equipment

Bar
With Tablecloth
Or Runner

Mixers

Signature Cocktails
& Recipe Cards

Mixers

ice

Bitters, Vinegars,
Condiments, Syrups,
Tonics

ice

Glassware

Fruit &
Garnish

Stir Sticks,
Napkins,
Bar Picks

Fruit &
Garnish

Glassware

*Sample bar diagram for
a large crowd*

A great alternative to a table is to have a rolling bar cart or two. They are easily transported and truly decorative. If you have more than one, you can duplicate setups so that people don't have to crowd around one bar. And bear in mind that an eye-catching bar presentation has a positive psychological effect: everyone will think their drinks taste better. Your bar real estate is like beachfront property.

PARTY TRICK—Tailor an oversized cloth to your table by pinning the edges or using napkin rings to gather extra material at the corners. This gives it a finished look.

Choosing the Theme

Is your party casual or rustic? Elegant and upscale? The color scheme and the way you decorate the bar with centerpieces are important elements of the entertaining stage. Think about seasonal cocktail choices: lighter for warmer months, and heavier for colder seasons. Straight bourbon or on the rocks is a universal pleaser and is not bound by the weather. Complementary trays, ice buckets, bowls, and glassware add functionality as well as personality. You might be surprised what props you already have lying around the house that you can incorporate into the décor. Do the unexpected.

Signature cocktail served in a batch

Bartending

To bartend or not to bartend? Making individual drinks, especially for a thirsty crowd, can be like a ball and chain for the host. Hiring a bartender is the ideal solution when you have more than thirty guests, but the simplest (and fastest) way to appease a crowd is to make a signature cocktail and prepare a large batch in advance. The cocktail can be set out in decanters or ladled into glasses from a punch bowl. Another presentation that is always a crowd-pleaser is an infusion. Take a seasonal fruit or herb and let it soak in bourbon for at least twenty-four hours to marry the flavors. Serve over ice for a flavored, ready-made cocktail.

Peggy's husband hand-squeezes oranges whenever he concocts his whiskey sours, but it's a lot of work. If you have fewer than ten guests, go for it. Impress the crowd with the first round and then venture out from behind the bar and enjoy the party. You can create a self-serve bar by stocking it well and making periodic checks to replenish supplies.

To test a cocktail before serving, use the bartender's trick of dipping a straw to capture just a small taste and then make any necessary enhancements. We always taste before serving; it's one of the advantages of being the party host.

PARTY TRICK— You can use decanters, or you can save half a dozen empty bourbon bottles to hold batched cocktails and as décor.

Reused bourbon bottles serving as decorative decanters

There is nothing wrong with displaying several different styles of bourbon that vary in terms of mash bill (traditional rye or wheated), proof strength, or age. This allows guests to explore and discuss the delectable choices before they pour. It also shows that you are spirits savvy. There are hundreds of bourbon brands and many styles (see chapter 3). A simple pitcher of water should always be available for the bourbon splasher, as well as an ice bucket for those who prefer a slowly melting cube.

Every bourbon and cocktail creation has its own unique flavor and story. Have some fun and provide the name of the drink and its story on a place card so your guests can appreciate what they are drinking.

Choose several styles of bourbon and dress them up with decanters

Glassware

People wear glassware like they wear jewelry or cologne; personal preference speaks to their individual style. If a simple bourbon on the rocks is the drink of choice, have rocks glasses (also known as old-fashioned glasses) available. Manhattans call for a traditional stemmed cocktail glass or coupe glass. (Tip: Hold the glass by the stem and not by the bowl to avoid allowing your hand to warm the painstakingly chilled drink.) Those who enjoy their bourbon neat or with a tiny bit of water often prefer the Glencairn glass. It was developed in Scotland for tasting Scotch and has become the glass of choice for many whiskey lovers worldwide.

Set out trays on the bar holding different styles of glasses. This makes it easy to whisk away an empty tray and refill it with your backup supply. Line the tray with a napkin, so the glasses don't slip. Whatever kind of glassware you use—and it doesn't have to be fine crystal—don't worry about everything matching. Mixed glassware can be quite fun. Clear glasses showcase the beauty of a cocktail, but colored glasses or julep cups can certainly jazz up a bar.

PARTY TRICK—
Chill the glasses and mixers in the refrigerator before guests arrive. This will keep the drinks colder.

PARTY TRICK—
Susan cleans her glasses by hand using Alconox, a concentrated laboratory glassware cleaner that can be purchased online. After the clean glasses have drained for a few minutes, wipe them dry, inside and out, with a clean cloth or paper towels. This leaves the glasses sparkling and odor free. A four-pound box of the powdered detergent may seem expensive (more than $30), but it can last a decade. Otherwise, Dawn dishwashing liquid works well.

Use decorative chocolate cordial cups to hold small tastings

PARTY TRICK—
Use chocolate cordial cups for a surprise sip and built-in chocolate "chaser."

Old Fashioned		Cocktail glass	
Tall		Glencairn glass	
Champagne flute		Wine glass	
Shot glass		Mule mug	
Pint beer glass		Punch cup	

PARTY TRICK—
If you have only a
small icemaker or
don't have a lot of ice
cube trays, stock up
on ice the week of the
party and keep the
cubes in ziplock bags
in the freezer. Or
invest in a cooler and
buy bags of ice.

PARTY TRICK—
Display bar tools in a
small carafe or vase to
add visual interest and
to keep them easily
accessible.

Ice

Ice is the soul of the American cocktail and adds a delicate statement. Large block ice cubes melt slowly and usually last for a refill. Use smaller ice cubes for your cocktail shaker. Position an ice bucket with a scoop (or tongs) at an easy-to-reach angle. Check periodically throughout the evening to ensure that the ice in the bucket hasn't melted, and refill as needed. Using two ice buckets per bar means that replenishing can wait a little longer.

Bar Equipment Basics

Bar equipment ranges from spoons to muddlers to shakers. No one expects you to have twenty pieces of equipment like a professional mixologist. Keep it simple, and think about what you need for your cocktail selections. Keep a small paring knife handy for wax-top bottles and bar fruit, along with a cutting board. Mixing spoons and measuring pourers are a must. Other essentials include the following:

Bar spoon with long handle
Glass mixing beaker
Citrus reamer or stripper
Cocktail shakers (small and large)
Mini grater
Strainer
Jigger (1 ounce and 2 ounce)
Muddler
Ice bucket
Ice scoop
Ice tongs
Foil and wax cutter (or small knife)
Bottle stoppers
Biodegradable straws and picks

Sample bar-tool collection

Mixers and Condiments

Mixers and condiments can be kept together on small trays. This helps keep the bar organized. Or you can put fruit, such as cherries or orange slices, in small bowls. (We highly recommend Luxardo or Bada Bing cherries—expensive, but worth it!)

The standard mixers are club soda (or sparkling water) and ginger ale. Have sweet vermouth for Manhattans, as well as bitters. If you want to serve Kentucky mules (see the recipe on page 123), have ginger beer on hand, too. For guests who prefer nonalcoholic drinks, have chilled bottles of flavored water.

In general, clear cocktails are stirred, and creamy cocktails are shaken. A bartender taught us a long time ago to shake a cocktail until the froth, or chill, can be seen on the outside of the shaker. That is how you know it's ready to pour.

PARTY TRICK—Soak sugar cubes in different flavors of bitters and set them out on individual trays. Be sure to label which bitters have been used for which cubes. These add a wonderful twist to old-fashioneds.

Sugar cubes soaked in orange and walnut bitters

PARTY TRICK—Lay a rocks glass sideways on a stack of napkins. Turn it clockwise to fan the napkins for a great presentation.

Lay a glass on stacked napkins and twist for a fanned look

Decorative napkin presentation

Glass rimming

Bar Nibbles

Keep something savory or salty (nuts, pretzels, or cheddar crackers) in a small dish on the bar. Nibbling gives people something to do while they wait for their drinks.

Garnish

Garnish is the grand finale of the cocktail. Prepare seasonal garnishes well in advance if slicing is required, and assemble them in bowls or compartments for easy access. In a garnish, we look for the appropriate size, flavor, and color to complement the cocktail. Remember that the garnish is there to enhance the cocktail, not compete with it. Keep herbs hydrated in a glass of water until you're ready to use them, so they stay springy and fresh. Spears, straws, and rimming sugars or seasonings can

> **PARTY TRICK—** Set up the nibbles as food pairings with an assortment of bourbons (see chapter 4).

	JAN	FEB	MAR	APR	MAY	JUN	JUL	AUG	SEP	OCT	NOV	DEC
Apples												
Apricots												
Blackberries												
Blueberries												
Cantaloupe												
Cherries												
Cranberries												
Figs												
Grapefruit												
Grapes												
Honeydew												
Mangoes												
Nectarines												
Oranges												
Papayas												
Peaches												
Pears												
Pineapple												
Plums												
Raspberries												
Rhubarb												
Strawberries												
Tangerine												
Watermelon												

Seasonal garnish chart

PARTY TRICK—Don't refrigerate whole fruit before slicing it; this tightens the pulp and makes it less juicy. Roll the fruit on the counter before slicing to enhance the juiciness. Strain fruit juices to remove seeds and pulp. Lemons and limes tend to turn bitter overnight, so it's best to slice them on the day of the party.

be displayed in decorative ways. If you dip the rim in fruit juice, this makes it easier for the rimming sugar to stick to the glass. Or you can circle the rim with fresh fruit.

What's the "Proper" Way to Serve Bourbon?

God forbid that anyone should drink a wee dram of Scotch without a splash of water. Kilts would ruffle. And the myriad rules for wine are exhausting. Happily, there is no need to obsess about the proper way to serve bourbon. The fabulous fact is that the bourbon industry made our native American spirit approachable a long time ago. The undeniably gracious master distillers of Kentucky simply want you to enjoy their products without pretense. As Fred Noe of Jim Beam puts it, "Drink it any way you damn well please." We give that sentiment a "Hell yeah" and a "Halleluiah." The only truly important question is how each guest enjoys his or her bourbon.

You get the point. There are no rules, except to drink responsibly. Oscar Wilde once said, "As a host you have a moral obligation to be interesting." Agreed. But if you set up your bourbon bar the right way, you will be forgiven just about anything.

THREE

How to Do a Bourbon Tasting

VANILLA OR CARAMEL. Cherries or peaches. Cinnamon or nutmeg. Almonds or pecans. These may sound like choices for a recipe, and in a way, they are. These flavors and many, many more are commonly detectable in bourbon. Distillers carefully craft their spirits with certain flavor profiles in mind. A bourbon tasting can offer a tantalizing mix of mystery and hints of the familiar. We all know how an apple tastes, but would we expect to encounter that flavor in a glass of whiskey?

With decades of experience introducing people to bourbon, we know how to heighten your senses. Everyone comes to the table with food memories, and the flavors encountered in bourbon are those from your fruit bin, bread box, spice cabinet, and secret cache of candy. Whether you and your guests are new to bourbon or seasoned enthusiasts, your party will be energized by a bourbon tasting. Participants will debate which fruit, nut, and spice flavors they can detect. One person's apple may be another's pear. Which is a better descriptor, corn or corn bread? Your guests will ask questions. They will vote on favorites. In short, they will have a great time, and your party will be talked about for weeks—or longer.

What Is Bourbon?

All bourbon is whiskey, which is defined as a distilled spirit made from a fermented cereal grain or a "beer." The beer is distilled at no higher than 190 proof, and then the spirit is placed in an oak container to age. Once it is removed from the oak, whiskey must be bottled at no less than 80 proof. That's the definition of basic whiskey (or in Scotland, whisky). Different styles have various recipe, proof, and aging requirements.

In 1964 Congress declared bourbon "a distinctly American product." Just as a sparkling wine made outside of the Champagne region of France cannot be called champagne, corn-based whiskey made outside of the United States cannot be called bourbon. Here's what has to happen for a whiskey to be bourbon:

- It has to be made from a mash bill (recipe) of at least 51 percent corn. Most bourbons are about 75 percent corn. Other grains (called "smalls") such as malted barley, rye, and wheat may be used as well.
- Bourbon cannot be distilled at higher than 160 proof.

- Bourbon must be stored in a brand-new charred, white oak container (almost always a 53-gallon barrel) at no more than 125 proof. Only pure water can be added to adjust the proof. No other additives are allowed. (In Scotland and Canada, distillers are permitted to add caramel coloring to whiskey.)
- Bourbon has to be bottled at a minimum of 80 proof (40 percent alcohol by volume).
- Bourbon has to be a product of the United States.

Bourbon has no age requirement. As soon as the distillate touches the wood of the barrel, it is "bourbon." There are, however, some rules about aging that must be followed for whiskey to qualify as "straight bourbon": the bourbon has to be aged for at least two years in a new oak container (almost always a barrel, but sometimes smaller than the standard 53 gallons). If the distiller wants to bottle the bourbon without an age statement, the whiskey inside has to be at least four years old; otherwise, the label must state the time spent aging, such as "Two Years, 16 Months." You may see a label that says "Bottled-in-Bond." This designation dates from a law passed in 1897 to ensure whiskey quality. The short version of the law's provisions is that the whiskey must be made at a single distillery (not sourced from several different distilleries and batched), made during a single distilling season (six months), aged no less than four years, and bottled at no younger than four years old.

Bourbon-Tasting Basics

For a basic tasting, you should probably have no more than three bourbons. Even two can work well, especially if they have very different flavor profiles. The recipes for bourbon fall into three major categories: traditional (corn making up three-quarters to four-fifths of the mash bill, with rye and malted barley constituting the rest), wheated (wheat used in place of rye in the mash bill), and high rye (corn percentage only about two-thirds). Here are some examples:

Traditional	*Wheated*	*High Rye*
Blanton's	Larceny	Basil Hayden
Buffalo Trace	Maker's Mark	Bulleit
Evan Williams	Old Fitzgerald	Four Roses "B" recipe
Knob Creek	Rebel Yell	Old Grand-Dad
Michter's US*1	W. L. Weller	Redemption
Wild Turkey		
Woodford Reserve		

PARTY TRICK— Don't use fragrant flowers as a centerpiece because their strong scent will interfere with the aroma of the bourbon.

Slate plates used to present the tasting

Of course, all bourbons are distinctive, but most people will be able to notice marked differences when you choose bourbons from two or three of these categories.

Glassware

Tulip-shaped glasses are preferred, whether you use small wineglasses or Glencairn whiskey glasses. The bulb shape helps release the aromatics in the bourbon, and the relatively narrow throat or chimney traps and concentrates them near the lip of the glass.

If you are hosting more than a handful of guests, you may want to provide just one tasting glass to each participant. Each person should rinse her or his glass with water between tastes and drink the water, which serves the dual purpose of cleaning the glass and cleaning the palate. Plus, one glass per person means less glassware to be washed later!

Tasting Mats

Tasting mats are especially useful if you are prepouring the samples. In addition to reserving a space for each sample, the mats can provide information about each bourbon, such as distillery, proof, and mash bill.

PARTY TRICK— Pour the bourbon within twenty minutes of your guests' arrival. Each sample should be no more than a quarter of an ounce—about a "finger."

SET GLASS HERE   SET GLASS HERE   SET GLASS HERE

Old Forester
86°
No Age Statement
72% Corn, 18% Rye,
10% Malted Barley
Brown-Forman Distillery
Louisville, KY

Maker's Mark
90°
No Age Statement
Wheated Mashbill
Maker's Mark Distillery,
Loretto, KY

Bulleit
90°
At least 6 years.
High Rye Mashbill
Bulleit Distillery
Shelbyville, KY

Sample basic tasting mat

Depending on the tasters' level of experience, you can use either a basic mat (see the sample provided) or one with more detailed information (see chapter 5).

Nibbles

Certain foods pull out different components of a whiskey's flavor. Have little dishes of the following on hand for the tasting. Use them, in the order listed, for the first bourbon you taste. Doing this will help you understand the major flavor components.

Food	Effect
Dried cherries or cranberries	Enhances the fruit notes
Pecans	Enhances oak tannins
Milk chocolate pieces	Brings out chocolate and/or vanilla notes
Chewy caramel candy	Blends all the elements back together
Oyster crackers or unsalted crackers	Helps cleanse the palate between bourbons

Bourbon Facts

Bourbon is not just a spirit. It's a lifestyle. It's impossible to appreciate bourbon without understanding a bit of its history. At the beginning of the tasting, take a few minutes to give your guests some of this background.

More than 90 percent of bourbon comes from Kentucky. The Bluegrass State's master distillers have a treasure trove of the world's finest ingredients. Calcium-rich limestone-filtered water is one of the hallmarks of fine bourbon (and the key to strong bones in Kentucky Thoroughbreds). The water is iron free, so the whiskey will not have a bitter flavor and will not turn black (a great color for coffee, but not for whiskey). The high mineral content also gives the yeast a nutritional boost as it carries out the important function of fermentation.

Bourbon must be at least 51 percent corn, which is largely responsible for establishing its flavor. (If bourbon is sweeter than other whiskeys, consider that corn bread is sweeter than other breads.) Rye or wheat and malted barley are also part of the mash bill the distiller uses to create the bourbon.

Yeast adds a delicious nuttiness, as well as fruit and floral aromas. Distilleries' yeast strains are proprietary, and some date back to the 1800s. A yeast strain may determine whether the fruit note in a bourbon is apples, pears, peaches, or something else. Sweet spice notes, such as cinnamon, also come from certain yeast strains.

PARTY TRICK— Pour a few drops of bourbon in your hand and then rub your hands together. Smell your palms. You will detect a marked grain aroma similar to that of bread or cereal.

Sample presentation of a tasting for a group

PARTY TRICK—
The effect of wood can be illustrated by soaking toothpicks overnight in a small glass of water. By the next day, the water will have picked up the woodiness.

Age matters. That's why master distillers are patient and very particular about the amount of time they age their whiskey in barrels, like steeping a tea bag in water. The longer the maturation process, the richer the color and the deeper the wood notes pulled from the barrel. White oak barrels act like large blocks of sugar, releasing vanillin (vanilla). Once the inside of the barrel is charred and toasted, the wood sugar is caramelized, like the topping of a crème brûlée. All the color and most of the flavor of bourbon come from its time in the barrel. Older is not necessarily better, though. Thanks to hot Kentucky summers, a lot of evaporation occurs during aging. Bourbons in their teens risk becoming tannic. That said, some very old bourbons are very good indeed. But you pay a premium for them because there is less whiskey in a fifteen- to twenty-year-old barrel than in a seven-year-old barrel. For every year of aging, about 5 percent of the whiskey is lost to evaporation.

The lowest-proof bourbon is 80 proof (40 percent alcohol). A higher proof may add complexity, but it may also "lock up" some of the flavors with the alcohol. Adding a few drops of water can "open up" a higher-proof bourbon to reveal multiple flavor layers, especially the fruity notes.

Barrel flavor notes by Independent Stave

A good rule of thumb for tasting is to start with the lowest-proof bourbon and proceed to the highest.

All these factors contribute to bourbon's complexity—what we call following the flavor map of spice, sweet, savory, fruit, and earthy—and they are key to any great bourbon. Generally, the higher the quality, the more complex it is.

The Tasting Steps

When tasting, there are four things to consider: color, aroma, flavor, and finish. That's easy enough, but you have to go beyond flavor and consider complexity to determine how to pair a particular bourbon with a specific food (examined in detail in the next chapter).

STEP 1—COLOR. Every bourbon gets its depth of color from the barrel in which it was aged. In general, light-colored bourbon has matured for fewer years than dark-colored bourbon. However, if a barrel has a very dark char, even a relatively young bourbon may have a rich color. Each distillery chooses the amount of toasting (how long the wood staves are heated) and the char (blistering of the interior of the barrel with an intense flame).

The toasted layer (also called the red layer) is where the bourbon picks up all its color and much of its flavor during aging. Toasting can be light or dark, just as you can set the level on your kitchen toaster. The char blisters the wood so the whiskey can easily move in and out of the red layer. During hot summers, the wood expands, and the whiskey migrates into the red layer. The cold of winter causes the wood to contract, and the bourbon is squeezed back into the barrel.

Examine the glass against a white background (a tablecloth or napkin works well). Look for a rich amber color that has sparkle and bounce. View the bourbon for clarity and delicate highlights. Note the following colors:

Yellowish	Reddish
Light straw	Light straw
Straw	Copper penny
Dark straw	Bronze
Honey	

STEP 2—AROMA. Trust your nose! It is responsible for 75 percent of your flavor perception. You might feel compelled to dive into all the possible flavors of bourbon. But especially in the case of higher-proof bourbons, don't overwhelm your sense of smell by putting your nose too

far into the glass. Instead, rest the glass under or to the side of your nose and move the glass toward you and away from you as you distinguish the aromas. Bourbon aromas tend to have layers. At first nose, many people notice the vanilla and caramel; then you can try to go deeper.

After the first nosing, turn your head and "blow away" the scent through your mouth. Now nose again. You'll find that the initial hit of alcohol in the first nosing is gone and you can smell the other aromatics. Be aware of the spices, fruits, nuts, and other aromatics; take your guests through each category and ask them what they detect. These aromas define the structure. Add a drop or two of water to release fruit notes and reveal hidden aromatics.

PARTY TRICK—
If you experience "nose fatigue"—that is, if all you can smell is alcohol—pause and sniff the back of your hand or the cloth of your sleeve. Or sniff fresh whole coffee beans, which can also refresh the olfactory sense.

Nosing a glass

Tasting the bourbon

STEP 3—FLAVOR AND MOUTHFEEL. After building the anticipation of aroma, the best part, of course, is tasting! Let a small amount of bourbon rest on your tongue and then, as we say in Kentucky, "chew" on it. Some bourbons coat your tongue, while others seem thin. This is the mouthfeel. The flavors will astound you as you focus on the sensation of the whiskey in your mouth. Unlike wine tasters, who pull air into the mouth, you want to blow air out of your mouth to break down the alcohol and get to the core of the flavors. As described earlier, try the fruit, nut, chocolate, and caramel nibbles in sequence for the first bourbon in your tasting. This will help you tease out the flavor layers. If you like, you can do this with the other bourbons in your flight (tasting), but it's not necessary. We recommend cleansing the palate with oyster crackers and water between whiskeys. Above all, relax and enjoy the flavors!

STEP 4—FINISH. Peggy's father used to say, "A great bourbon will 'wrap' your tongue like a satin ribbon." The taste is rich and warm. The finish, or aftertaste, may be dry and sweet or spicy and bold. The true test is whether the finish lingers as if the liquid were still in your mouth. The longer it lingers, the better quality the bourbon. If you return to the empty glass later and there is a lingering aroma, that's the sign of a good bourbon.

TYPICAL BOURBON AROMA AND FLAVOR DESCRIPTORS

BASIC

Caramel (and variations, including toffee and praline)

Vanilla (and variations such as crème brûlée and vanilla icing)

BREAD/YEAST

Corn bread

Cornmeal

Malty

Rye

Warm cereal

Yeasty dough

FRUITY

Apple (ripe, green, baked)

Apricot

Banana

Berry (raspberry, blueberry, strawberry, currant)

Cherry

Citrus (orange, orange peel, lemon, lime, grapefruit)

Date

Fig

Grape (wine notes, especially if finished in wine casks)

Peach

Pear

Plum

Raisin

SPICES

Allspice

Anise

Black pepper

Cayenne

Cinnamon

Clove

Fennel

Ginger

Licorice

Nutmeg

White pepper

SUGAR/SWEET

Butterscotch

Chocolate—dark, milk, white

Honey

Maple

Marzipan

Sorghum

Sugared dates

Toffee

FLORAL

Dried flowers/potpourri

Geranium

Hibiscus

Honeysuckle

Lavender

Lilac

Orange blossom

Peach blossom

Rose

HERBAL

Black tea

Celery

Dill

Green pepper

Green tea

Mint

Parsley

Rosemary

Sage

Sassafras

Tobacco

NUTTY/WOODY

Almond

Coconut

Coffee

Hazelnut

Macadamia

Oak/cedar

Pecan

Pine

Walnut

Wood smoke

EARTHY

Biscuit

Corn husk

Egg

Grass/hay/straw

Leather

Leaves

Mushroom

Roasted vegetables

Potpourri tray of sensory food for an elegant presentation

There Are No Wrong Answers

No single bourbon has *all* the aromas and flavors in the accompanying list of descriptors. But better bourbons are usually more complex and encompass a greater number of them. The most important thing to remember is that you are *tasting*, not *drinking*. Take small sips, and pay attention. The larger your "flavor vocabulary," the better your ability to describe what you are tasting. For example, there may be a note of butterscotch in the bourbon, but if you've never had butterscotch, you won't have a word for the flavor you're tasting. And remember (we cannot emphasize this enough), everyone's palate is different. One person's cinnamon may be another's nutmeg.

For basic tastings and for people who are not familiar with bourbon, you may want to provide some sample descriptors from the list. Having multiple options to choose from is easier than pulling adjectives out of the air! If you and your guests want to take an even deeper dive into bourbon flavors, or if you are experienced whiskey lovers, you can use a more advanced tasting mat and rate the intensity of each type of flavor.

Examples of Flights

Once you have hosted a basic tasting, subsequent parties can be centered around bourbon themes. Try tasting bourbons that are the same proof, bourbons aged more than ten years, or bourbons of the same style (traditional, wheated, or high rye), or compare bourbons to Scotch, Irish, or Tennessee whiskeys.

Age

Taste the bourbons in order from youngest to oldest. You'll have to find bourbons with age statements on their labels, which is a little harder than it used to be, since many distilleries have dropped age statements. However, if a bourbon is less than four years old, the age *must* be included on the label (you may see "Two Years" or "36 Months"). Here are some bourbons that still display age statements: Very Old Barton (6 years), Old Ezra (7 years), Knob Creek (9 and 12 years), Henry McKenna Bottled-in-Bond (10 years), I. W. Harper (12 and 15 years), and Elijah Craig (12 and 18 years). Also, many private selections that can be found at retailers have age statements. For example, bottles of Four Roses Private Barrel Selections give the age in years and months, such as "11 Years, 3 Months."

Barrel Proof (Cask Strength)

These bourbons have not had their proofs adjusted with distilled water before bottling. They always benefit from the addition of a little water during tasting to tame the alcohol heat and unlock the flavor layers. Examples are Booker's, Elijah Craig Single Barrel, Four Roses Single Barrel Private Select, Maker's Mark Cask Strength, Old Forester 1920, Stagg Jr., and Wild Turkey Rare Breed.

American Whiskey Styles

Besides bourbon, the other main styles of American whiskey are Tennessee whiskey and rye. Tennessee whiskey (made exclusively in the Volunteer State) has the same mash-bill requirement as bourbon: it has to be at least 51 percent corn. But there is an extra step in the process of making Tennessee whiskey. After coming off the still, it is filtered through sugar-maple charcoal for smoothness before being put in barrels to age. These whiskeys tend to have a higher corn content than bourbon, resulting in a sweeter flavor profile. Widely available Tennessee whiskeys are Jack Daniels and George Dickel.

Rye whiskey is required to have a mash bill that is at least 51 percent rye (a few are 100 percent rye); the other grains are usually corn and malted barley. Many Kentucky distilleries make rye, including Peerless, Wild Turkey, Heaven Hill (Rittenhouse is the brand), Bulleit, Beam (Knob Creek Rye and others), Buffalo Trace (Sazerac Rye), and Old Forester. This style of whiskey is more traditionally associated with the mid-Atlantic states. Good examples from outside Kentucky are Sagamore Spirit, Catoctin Creek (Roundstone Rye), Dad's Hat, and McKenzie Straight Rye.

International Whiskey Styles

This can get complicated, but the main thing to know is that most whiskeys produced outside of North America are barley based. These include Scotch, Irish, and Japanese whiskeys. Canadian whiskey is based on rye.

Scotch is a vast category, and many books have been devoted to this style of whiskey. It can be fruity, smoky, or peaty; in the case of Scotch distilled on islands, it can even contain the tang of the sea. Irish whiskeys tend to be lighter and more floral in character than either American or Scotch whiskeys. Japanese whiskeys are generally very similar to Scotch types. For a very basic comparative tasting, we suggest that you choose your favorite bourbon and then pick one of the following from each type and taste in order: bourbon, Canadian, Irish, Scotch.

Canadian: Caribou Crossing, Crown Royal, Lot No. 40, Seagram's VO, Whistle Pig (bottled in Vermont but made in Canada).

Irish: Bushmill's Original, Midleton Very Rare, Redbreast (any age), Tullamore Dew (aged expressions).

Scotch: Johnnie Walker Black, a benchmark blended Scotch with a little peat; nonpeated Glenfiddich or Glenmorangie; Talisker or Laphroaig for lots of smoky peat.

Geographic Region or State

Bourbon is now being made in every state, although the vast majority still comes from Kentucky. Check the shelves of your local retailer to see what is available. We think it's fun to do a blind tasting with three bourbons—one from Kentucky and two from other states—and see whether the participants can spot the Kentucky product. Use your favorite Kentucky bourbon. Some of the "outsiders" we can recommend are Balcones Texas Blue Corn (Texas), Bowman Brothers (Virginia), F. E. W. (Chicago), Hudson Baby (New York), J. Henry & Sons (Wisconsin), and Wyoming Whiskey (Wyoming).

Note that many bourbons from distilleries in Kentucky and Indiana are bottled by companies located elsewhere. There is absolutely nothing wrong with this, and many of these brands from nondistiller producers are excellent. But double-check the label (usually the back one) because you may think a bottle was distilled in Colorado or Florida or California and see "Distilled in Kentucky" in the fine print. Again, that doesn't mean it isn't very good, but it won't be useful for your geographic comparison.

BOURBONS
BY STYLE

TRADITIONAL — HIGH RYE — WHEATED

BOURBONS
BY GEOGRAPHY

Statesville, NC — Chicago, IL — Kirby, WY

BARREL
STRENGTH

127.4 — 129.5 — 131.4

FOUR

Food Pairings and Cooking with Bourbon

HOW-TOS FOR ANY OCCASION

PEGGY LOVED GRILLED CHEESE AS A CHILD, and Kraft made it easy to love. It was fun to unwrap those little orange squares of delight. Happily, our tastes evolve and mature. One Christmas, Peggy experienced the epiphany of Gouda. (Wow! So *this* is cheese.) It was so much better than those precious orange slices, and it opened the floodgates to exploring other varieties—goat, blue, Camembert, and beyond. She had a similar experience with bourbon: she was introduced to it in college—probably not the top-shelf version—but she knew she liked it.

With bourbon, the more you sample, the more your taste buds want to experience all the robust, complex styles of bourbon. So with that in mind, we would like to introduce you to the foundation of bourbon and food pairings. Anyone can educate his or her taste, taking it from basic to advanced, whether the subject is whiskey, foods, or the two together.

More often than not, bourbon lovers are also foodies, eager to explore what works together. To get started, all you need are your kitchen and your sense of taste. Peggy is a master taster, and Susan is an executive bourbon steward, but that doesn't mean our taste buds are better than yours—we just have a lot of experience. We learn every time we "practice" (and we practice a lot) tasting and evaluating new spirits and foods together. Think of it as calisthenics for your palate. You are developing its "food memory." As we noted earlier, if you have never tasted butterscotch, you won't be able to recognize and identify that flavor in a bourbon. But if butterscotch is in your flavor vocabulary, you will know it when you taste it.

When we describe bourbon tasting notes, we use terms for food flavors, such as spicy, sweet, savory, and herbal. You are already familiar with these flavors from your spice rack, the meats and fruits in your refrigerator, and various pantry items such as nuts, crackers, and other snacks.

The Flavor Trio

More than fifteen years ago, Peggy created one of the first food and bourbon pairing wheels with chef David Larson. Their intention was not to teach people to appreciate bourbon and food pairings; they simply wanted to spread the bourbon gospel. Fast-forward, and this method

has evolved into a teaching tool for audiences everywhere. There's no better way to begin than by training the palate through an easy and enjoyable process. The technique is called *balance, counterbalance,* and *explosion,* and happily, you can use it in your own home.

Balance results when the flavors of a bourbon match the flavor of a food. *Counterbalance* occurs when a completely opposite food flavor highlights certain bourbon flavor profiles. Finally, *explosion* is what happens when the predominant flavor of a bourbon is matched with a predominant flavor in a food, leading to surround-sound flavor in your mouth—hence the explosion.

Combine the tasting food with the sample for a decorative presentation

A Food Pairing Party

So how do you throw a food pairing party? Start with the basics. Choose the bourbon first, to dissect the flavors. Once you have identified the flavors of the bourbon, select foods to balance, counterbalance, or explode those flavors.

For a simple party, you can pour your bourbons (roughly 2-ounce pours) up to thirty minutes in advance. Pouring the bourbon ahead of

time invites the whiskey to open a bit, allowing the complex flavors to emerge. You want to be able to taste the bourbon in pure form and then have enough left over to pair with the food. For basic pairings, choose a single-flavor food that is bite-sized and requires little preparation or refrigeration, so you can set up in advance. The layout of the offerings can be casual or elegant. The accompanying illustrations show basic settings using simple food.

Some of our favorite simple foods to pair with bourbon are nuts, dried or fresh fruit, chocolate, and cheese. To demonstrate the pairing process, we've used some of our favorite bourbons as examples. Elijah Craig has a nice, well-rounded, nutty pecan and caramel flavor, which is a perfect balance for pecans. Maker's Mark has wonderful honey and citrus notes, so an orange slice is ideal for balance. Old Forester's rich caramel note is counterbalanced by Parmesan, which is generally considered a topping and is a bit bland; the bourbon brightens the Parmesan and brings it to life. Four Roses Single Barrel has huge chocolate notes, and when it is paired with dark chocolate, you receive that flavor explosion of chocolate that is almost too much of a good thing!

For more advanced pairings with appetizers, you simply need to focus on the breakdown of the food flavors. Then ask yourself: how should the appetizer be constructed? Do you want to serve a toast point and cheese with chutney, or smoked pork with barbecue sauce on a medallion bun? Because bourbons are complex, try to identify the predominant flavors

Simple Food Pairings

Bourbon	Predominant Flavor	Food	Food Pairing Sensation
Elijah Craig	Pecan and caramel	Pecans	Balance
Maker's Mark	Citrus and honey	Orange slice	Balance
Four Roses Single Barrel	Chocolate, dark chocolate, and gingerbread	Dark chocolate	Explosion
Old Forester	Caramel, vanilla, and mature oak	Parmesan slice	Counterbalance

Cheese Options

Cheese	Structure	Flavor
Goat cheese or chèvre (French for "goat")	Airy and light; creamy	Citrusy and fresh; herbal and nutty (like hazelnuts); grassy
Parmesan	Shreds quickly and dissolves	Soft wood and pepper taste with a touch of nutmeg
Blue cheese	Robust and meaty; big bodied and lingers	Caramelized wood; intensely sweet

More Advanced Food Pairings

Bourbon	Flavor Profile	Balance	Counterbalance	Explosion
Maker's Mark	Honey Light citrus Soft grains and toast	Goat cheese Crostini Mandarin orange		
Woodford Reserve	Rich caramel Vanilla Soft pepper and dark fruit		Asian chili sauce Pork Parmesan wafer	
Baker's	Heavy caramel and smoke with nutty wood balance			Blue cheese with honey drizzle and walnuts Blackberries

*Baker's bourbon paired with blue cheese,
blackberries, and a honey drizzle*

Showcase your pairings on a stacked tray

of the bourbon and the appetizer, so you can choose to dial the flavors up or down.

Whichever style you prefer, take a bite of the food and then a sip of the bourbon, so the flavors can play together and create harmony. You may want to assemble a tray of food to accompany each pairing and unveil it as you proceed with the tasting, so the guests don't jump ahead to the next one before you're ready. Graduate the flavors of each food choice, so as not to tire your tongue from the first tasting to the last. For example, never start a pairing with a strong blue cheese or a spicy wasabi; it will alter your tasting experience and probably shut down your taste buds!

Atomizers for a quick tasting

Style and Accessories

Set the tone of your food pairing by expressing your personal style. The offerings can be displayed in several ways, depending on whether you're hosting an outdoor party, providing a tasting bar buffet, or setting up a small table in front of the fireplace. In the end, it all depends on what your guests' palates have to say, and that is where the fun happens! Here are the basics:

Bourbon—two or three unique styles, based on the flavor profile
Glassware—small glasses to trap the aroma of the bourbon
Place mats—to outline the names of the bourbons; leave room for tasting notes
Small plates—to hold the food
Water and water glasses—to add to the bourbon or for rinsing between tastings
Pens (optional)—for guests to write down their tasting notes
Whiskey spritzer or mister—for guests who want to explore without going too heavy on the palate
Dump bucket (optional)—for guests who choose not to swallow the bourbon

The Bourbon Pairing Buffet

For large parties, a true bourbon buffet of flavor vignettes is ideal, especially if the host won't be leading the tasting but still wants the guests to appreciate the pairings. Aligning the bourbon on trays or stations that accompany the generous food offerings is a great presentation and a real conversation piece.

Printed or handwritten cards that describe the bourbons and the food selections are informative, and they give your guests time to graze the buffet choices and pairings as they read. Although it is always a good idea to think about

Corn bread with a rich caramel drizzle assembled on a tray lined with dark pebbles

Antipasto tray with a bourbon chiffonade dressing

PARTY TRICK—
Divide your buffet
into individual tasting
stations for each
bourbon. This breaks
up the buffet line. Be
creative and repurpose
furniture in your home,
such as china cabinets,
armoires, coffee tables,
and chests, for the
tasting stations.

the color of the food on display, don't get hung up on the color scheme. You want the presentation to pop nicely side by side, but it is often most useful to set up the display according to the bourbon's style and proof.

If setting out whole bottles of bourbon is not cost-effective, you can use a whiskey spritzer or mister. This saves quite a bit of whiskey and prevents wasted pours that were not finished by your guests because the bourbons weren't their favorites. The spritzer is also helpful when you are deciding on your food pairings and don't want to swallow as you go during the testing and tasting process. Just spray twice in your mouth, and you will be able to dissect the notes. Then place the food in your mouth to marry the flavors.

Cooking with Bourbon

Bourbon has a stronger flavor and a higher alcohol content than wine, but don't be afraid to cook with it. You will find that it is one of the most versatile condiments and accents in your kitchen.

Because of bourbon's beautiful complexity and strong vanilla notes, we substitute it for vanilla in recipes calling for that ingredient. Marinades wake up when bourbon is added, and it heightens earthy notes in meat. Finally, reductions and sauces become more inviting because bourbon adds its layers of flavors.

Cooking with high-proof bourbon shouldn't be intimidating if you've cooked with brandy or wine. The key is to add the bourbon to a pan that is warm but not too hot. To be on the safe side, remove the pan from the heat before adding the whiskey. As the pan heats up, the alcohol evaporates, leaving behind wonderfully concentrated flavors as the sauce reduces.

Between the two of us, we have been pairing food with bourbon for more than half a century, and we are still learning every day how to do it with style. Not every dish you make needs to include bourbon, but those that don't (such as mashed or baked potatoes) make the whiskey-infused ones seem even more flavorful. Here are a few of our favorite recipes.

Appetizers and Small Bites

⟿ *Stuffed Mushroom Hors d'oeuvres with Henry Bain's Sauce*

Makes 24

This is the perfect bite-sized finger food, and it is simple to make. Henry Bain's sauce, created by the headwaiter at Louisville's Pendennis Club in the early twentieth century, is available from Bourbon Barrel Foods (see the appendix).

1 pound ground pork
1 teaspoon bourbon
2 teaspoons finely chopped fresh flat-leaf parsley
24 large white mushrooms, stems removed
Henry Bain's sauce

Preheat the oven to 350 degrees. Sauté the ground pork, bourbon, and parsley in a skillet until browned. Drain off the rendered fat. Place the mushrooms on a flat baking sheet and stuff each with a generous dollop of the ground meat mixture. Top each with ½ teaspoon of Henry Bain's sauce. Bake for 10 minutes.

⟿ *Kentucky Farm-Style Popcorn*

Makes about 3 cups

Susan's mother, Harriett, grew up on a farm in west-central Kentucky. Her family popped corn in bacon fat, since there was always plenty on hand after frying the bacon they made from butchering their own hogs. (Harriett's family also smoked their own hams and ground and seasoned their own sausage.) Not surprisingly, this method makes the popcorn taste like bacon (what could be better?). Susan has updated the technique by adding oil, which has a higher smoking point, to the bacon fat. This results in crunchy corn with a savory coating—no butter necessary. (Tip: Save bacon drippings in a ceramic mug kept in the refrigerator. You never know when you might want to add some extra bacony flavor to a recipe.)

¼ cup grape-seed oil
¼ cup bacon fat
¼ teaspoon bourbon
⅓ cup popcorn
Salt to taste
Dried dill (optional)

Over medium-high heat, combine the oil, bacon fat, and bourbon in a heavy-bottomed saucepan. When the surface begins to shimmer, add the popcorn and cover with a lid. Continuously shake the pan back and forth on the burner until the kernels stop popping. Dump the popped corn into a big bowl, sprinkle with salt, and serve. For added flavor, sprinkle with dried dill.

Antipasto Tray

Think of this as Kentucky meets Italy. You'll want to provide guests with toothpicks or small forks to spear the meat, cheese, and vegetables from the tray. If your buffet can accommodate only one tray, this one offers a good variety of bites.

NIBBLES
  ½ pound sliced salami
  ½ pound lightly cooked asparagus spears
  ½ pound cubed mozzarella
  Cherry tomatoes

CHIFFONADE DRESSING
  ¼ cup basil
  1 cup balsamic vinegar
  ½ cup sugar
  Juice of 1 lemon wedge
  ½ cup bourbon

Combine all the ingredients for the dressing in a jar and shake to mix. Drizzle some of the mixture on the food, and use the remainder for dipping.

Entrées

Granny Hunter's Bourbon Tenderloin

Serves 12

This elegant entrée comes from Peggy's mother-in-law, who entertained on the family farm in Bourbon County, Kentucky. It's a perfect example of a bourbon-enhanced marinade that doubles as a sauce.

2 tablespoons Kentucky bourbon
¾ cup vegetable oil
½ cup soy sauce
⅓ cup packed brown sugar
¼ cup red-wine vinegar
2 cloves garlic, peeled and minced
2 teaspoons ground ginger
½ teaspoon ground coriander
5- to 6-pound beef tenderloin

Combine all the ingredients in a baking dish or roaster large enough to hold the tenderloin. Marinate the meat in the refrigerator for 8 hours. Remove the marinade from the dish and boil it for 5 minutes. Pour it back over the tenderloin and bake in a 425-degree oven for 30 minutes. Reduce the heat to 375 degrees and bake another 20 minutes. Let the meat rest for about 10 minutes before slicing. Serve with warm marinade spooned over each slice.

You can substitute pork tenderloin for the beef. Sear the pork in a skillet to brown it before baking in a 350-degree oven for 30 minutes per pound.

Susan's Chicken and Country Ham Crêpes with Bourbon Cream Sauce

Serves 6

Slightly salty country ham is a great partner for tender chicken, and the bourbon in the cream sauce is a natural companion to both meats. Serve each guest two of these rich crêpes, along with a salad, some crusty bread, and an oak-aged wine (your choice—red or white).

CRÊPES
   ¾ cup milk
   ¾ cup water
   1 egg plus 1 egg yolk
   4 tablespoons melted butter (unsalted)
   1 cup white flour
   ½ teaspoon salt

Stir together the milk, water, eggs, and butter in a small mixing bowl. (Tip: If you use warm water and heat the milk in the microwave for 15 seconds, the melted butter won't harden upon contact with the cold ingredients.) In a second, larger mixing bowl, mix the flour and salt, then slowly whisk in the liquid ingredients until you have a smooth batter.

Lightly grease a nonstick 6-inch crêpe pan with a little butter. Over medium heat, add ¼ cup of batter and swirl to coat the pan. When bubbles on the surface start to break, flip the crêpe and cook the other side. Turn the cooked crêpe onto a plate and repeat, making a stack of cooked crêpes.

FILLING
   2 cups chicken breast cut into inch-long strips
   3 tablespoons butter (unsalted)
   ½ teaspoon salt
   ½ teaspoon black pepper
   12 slices country ham

Preheat the oven to 325 degrees. Pat the chicken dry, so it will brown. Sauté in butter on medium-high heat, tossing until each piece is lightly browned on all sides. Sprinkle with salt and pepper.

Lay a slice of ham on each crêpe, add about ⅓ cup of chicken, and roll up. Arrange in a buttered baking pan and cover with foil. Bake 20 to 30 minutes.

BOURBON CREAM SAUCE
   1 cup Kentucky bourbon
   2 cups heavy cream
   4 tablespoons softened butter (unsalted)
   ½ teaspoon salt
   ½ teaspoon pepper

In a saucepan, combine the bourbon and cream and heat until it just begins to boil. Reduce heat. While whisking continuously, add pieces of butter until they are all melted. Add salt and pepper to taste. Immediately serve over the crêpes.

Serves 6

Many craft brewers around the country (not just in Kentucky) are aging their beer in used bourbon barrels. This is usually done with dark brews such as stouts and porters, but some lighter ales are aged this way too—notably, Kentucky Bourbon Barrel Ale from Lexington, which is what we use in this recipe. But if you can only find bourbon-barrel-aged stout, give it a try and substitute a butterflied leg of lamb or lamb chops for the pork tenderloin. We highly recommend using soy sauce, Worcestershire sauce, and salt and pepper from Bourbon Barrel Foods (see the appendix).

    2 pork tenderloins (2 to 3 pounds total)
    1 cup olive oil
    1 cup Bourbon Barrel Ale
    1 teaspoon dried mustard powder
    ½ cup lemon juice
    3 tablespoons Worcestershire sauce
    ½ cup soy sauce
    2 teaspoons salt
    2 teaspoons coarsely ground black pepper

Combine all the liquid ingredients and spices in a baking dish (large enough to hold the meat) and whisk. Pierce the meat all over with a fork and place it in the marinade. Marinate for several hours or overnight in the refrigerator. Remove from the refrigerator about an hour before cooking to allow the meat to reach room temperature.

Preheat the oven to 350 degrees and cook for 30 minutes per pound. This is also great when cooked on the grill. Allow the meat to rest for a few minutes before slicing. In the meantime, pour the marinade into a saucepan and boil to reduce slightly. This makes a flavorful sauce to serve over the meat.

Sides

⌒ *Acorn Squash with Bourbon*

Serves 6

Almost everyone in Kentucky adds bourbon to their Thanksgiving sweet potato casseroles. But bourbon is also a natural flavor enhancer for acorn and butternut squash. Acorn squash is used here because it makes a great individual serving presentation.

    3 acorn squash, halved, with seeds removed
    Salt to taste
    6 teaspoons brown sugar
    6 teaspoons butter
    6 teaspoons bourbon

Preheat the oven to 350 degrees. Place the squash halves on a baking sheet, sprinkle each half with salt, and add 1 teaspoon of brown sugar and 1 teaspoon of butter to each. Bake for 30 minutes.

Remove from the oven, pierce the squash flesh in several places with a knife without breaking the skin, and add 1 teaspoon of bourbon to each. Cover with aluminum foil, return to the oven, and bake for an additional 20 minutes (30 minutes if the squash are large).

⌒ *Bourbon Carrots with Walnuts*

Serves 6

Bourbon and carrots are about the same color, right? So they will surely pair well. They certainly taste great together, especially when accompanied by walnuts, which amplify the oaky notes in the bourbon. Susan confesses that she hates cooked carrots, but she loves this dish. See how bourbon makes everything better?

    1 pound medium-sized carrots
    ¾ cup water
    ½ teaspoon salt
    ¼ teaspoon brown sugar
    2 tablespoons chopped walnuts
    1 tablespoon bourbon
    1 teaspoon lemon juice
    ¼ cup butter
    Salt and pepper to taste

Clean and peel the carrots. Chop them into chunks and then whiz in a food processor until coarsely grated. Add the carrots to a skillet along with the water, salt, and brown sugar and bring to a boil. Cover and cook over low heat for about 10 minutes, shaking the pan occasionally to make sure the carrots don't burn. If they seem to be getting dry, add some more water.

While the carrots are cooking, add the walnuts, bourbon, lemon juice, butter, and salt and pepper to a saucepan and heat on a very low setting just until the flavors combine and the sauce heats through. Pour over the carrots and serve immediately. Because the alcohol doesn't evaporate during cooking, you should probably serve this to guests aged twenty-one and older.

⌒ Asparagus with Bourbon Hollandaise

Serves 6

This recipe comes from David Larson, who was Woodford Reserve Distillery's first chef in residence. Asparagus with hollandaise is a classic. Add bourbon, and it's brilliant. (Tip: Omit the tomato and try this sauce on eggs Benedict. A little bourbon at breakfast may make your day brighter!)

    2 pounds asparagus, peeled and trimmed
    1 stick unsalted butter
    3 egg yolks
    2 tablespoons fresh lemon juice
    1 tablespoon bourbon
    3 tablespoons chopped fresh tomato
    Salt and pepper to taste

Bring a large saucepan of water to a boil, add the asparagus, and return to a gentle boil. Cook until tender-crisp and bright green: 1 to 2 minutes for tiny spears, 3 to 5 for small ones, 5 to 8 for medium, and 10 to 12 for large. Remove the asparagus from the pot and drain on paper towels or a tea towel. If you want to serve the dish at room temperature, plunge the asparagus into an ice bath.

Melt the butter in a saucepan; then remove it from the heat and cool to room temperature.

Fill the bottom of a double boiler with water and bring it almost to a boil over high heat. Reduce the heat to low so the water is hot but not boiling. Combine the egg yolks, lemon juice, and bourbon in the top of the double boiler. Whisk until blended and cook over the hot water until smooth, whisking constantly. Add the melted butter gradually, whisking constantly. If the sauce separates or curdles at this point, add an ice cube and whisk briskly until it melts. This will bring the sauce back together. Add the tomato and season to taste with salt and pepper. Drizzle the sauce over the asparagus on a serving platter and serve immediately.

Desserts

∽ *Bourbon Pineapple Pound Cake*

Serves 8 to 10, depending on how you slice your cake

This is a very quick and easy yet elegant dessert. Be sure to use fresh pineapple, not canned. Good pound cake is available from bakeries or in the bakery department at groceries, so you don't have to bake one from scratch.

  1 cup brown sugar
  ¼ cup bourbon
  1 to 2 fresh pineapples, quartered and sliced
     in thick strips
  1 pound cake

Preheat the oven to 175 degrees. Mix the brown sugar and bourbon until it forms a thin paste. Lay the pineapple strips side by side in a baking dish. Brush the brown sugar mixture thickly on the pineapple strips. Put the dish in the oven and allow the mixture to melt over the pineapple until warm.

Lay the pineapple strips over slices of pound cake and ladle any extra juice over each slice. Serve immediately.

Bourbon pineapple pound cake with a bourbon pairing

⤳ *Bourbon Brownies*

Makes 9 brownies

Our friend Albert Schmid has written several books about cooking with bourbon (see the appendix). This one, from his *Kentucky Bourbon Cookbook*, showcases the peerless pairing of bourbon and chocolate.

½ cup chopped pecans
¾ cup bourbon
½ cup butter
½ cup margarine
10 ounces (10 squares) semisweet chocolate
1 cup granulated sugar
½ cup brown sugar, firmly packed
½ teaspoon salt
5 eggs
¼ cup unsweetened cocoa
1½ cups flour

Preheat the oven to 350 degrees. Place the pecans and bourbon in a small bowl and let it sit to allow the nuts to absorb the whiskey. After about 30 minutes, or when the bourbon has been reduced by half, remove the pecans and place them on a small baking sheet. Reserve the remaining bourbon. Toast the pecans in the oven for about 5 minutes.

Heat the butter, margarine, and chocolate in a double boiler until melted. Allow the mixture to cool to room temperature. Add the sugar, brown sugar, salt, eggs, and reserved bourbon. Whisk until the ingredients are well mixed. Add the cocoa and mix until it is totally incorporated. Stir in the flour and the toasted pecans.

Apply nonstick spray to an 8- by 8-inch pan and pour in the batter. Bake for about 25 minutes, or until a toothpick comes out clean. Cut into squares when cool.

⌒⌒ Buttery Bourbon Oatmeal Cookies

Makes about 2 dozen cookies

Another admirable bourbon cookbook is Lynn Marie Hulsman's *Bourbon Desserts*. It's the source of this terrific cookie recipe that brilliantly uses bourbon-infused cherries instead of raisins.

½ cup dried cherries
¾ cup bourbon, for soaking the cherries
½ cup granulated sugar
¼ cup dark brown sugar
½ cup (1 stick) unsalted butter, room temperature
¾ teaspoon pure vanilla extract
3 tablespoons bourbon
1 large egg, room temperature
½ cup all-purpose flour
1½ cups rolled oats
¼ cup almond flour
½ teaspoon baking powder
½ teaspoon baking soda

At least one day or up to two weeks in advance, combine the dried cherries and bourbon in a tightly lidded jar. Shake the jar briskly from time to time to infuse.

Preheat the oven to 350 degrees. Line two 9- by 13-inch baking sheets with parchment.

Using an electric mixer set on medium-high speed, cream together the granulated sugar, brown sugar, butter, vanilla, and bourbon. Beat until light and fluffy, about 3 minutes. Add the egg and beat 1 minute more.

In a large mixing bowl, whisk together the flour, oats, almond flour, baking powder, and baking soda. Add this dry mixture to the butter mixture a little at a time, beating about 1 minute after each addition.

Drain the cherries, reserving the liquid to sip straight or use in cocktails. (Lynn: You rock!) Add the cherries to the batter and beat until just combined, less than 1 minute.

Drop the batter by tablespoons onto the parchment-lined sheets, leaving about 2 inches between cookies. Bake for 10 to 12 minutes, or until golden brown.

Remove from the oven, set the baking sheets on wire racks, and cool for 5 minutes; then transfer the cookies directly to the racks to finish cooling.

Store in a cake safe or airtight tin for up to 10 days.

FIVE

Advanced Pairings for the Bourbon Food Fanatic

AS YOU LEARNED IN THE LAST CHAPTER, food pairings don't have to be intimidating if you employ the basic tools of balance, counterbalance, and explosion. It's easy and straightforward. However, there's usually at least one "food fanatic" at every party who wants to dive more deeply into bourbon and food flavors, pairing his or her culinary favorites with all styles of bourbon. And why not? A well-made cocktail can be a work of art, but we also adore a fabulous bourbon paired with a complementary culinary dish. You may be surprised by the culinary versatility of bourbon; it is extremely complex and can lead you down many flavorful paths. Cocktail dinners (no wine allowed!) are both playful and enjoyable. So let's prepare your palate for some over-the-top tastes and pairings for your next party.

Priming Your Palate

Bourbon is the foundation of a pairing, but when you dissect the components of the production process, it creates a mental image of where the flavors originated. We actually use this mental imagery when we critique and rate whiskeys around the United States. It helps us find both flaws and positive characteristics in the distilled products we taste. The best chefs we know always taste their ingredients before they cook, testing for freshness, mouthfeel, and harmony among flavors. We do the same when we do pairings.

MOUTHFEEL AND TEXTURE. Mouthfeel and texture are important because you want to think about how the bourbon feels in your mouth and what it might pair nicely with. We call this the structure. We use the following characteristics when profiling, which refer not to *flavor* but to *sensation,* or the feel on the tongue:

Soft—Feels like light oil, as if it glides.
Sharp—Feels like licorice, which can roughen your tongue.
Viscosity—Does it feel like gelatin, water, or soda? Is it heavy or soft?
Astringency—Causes your tongue to pucker.
Heat—Note the intensity of the flame and where it hits your tongue.
Cool—Feels minty and herbaceous.

Contributions of the Distilling Process

Component	Positive Aspects	Negative Aspects
Water	Clean; little or no mineral flavor	Metallic
Grains	Corn—sweet, fresh Rye—bite of spice, rye bread Wheat—soft granola Barley—grits and oatmeal	Moldy and bitter
Yeast	Nutty and fresh green apple or pear	Heavy; sour or bitter
Still	Clean and fresh	Burnt and rubbery
Barrel (wood)	Earthy and savory	
Proof	Heft and warmth	

INTENSITY. Weather is judged by intensity because there are so many variations in our weather patterns, and the same applies to bourbons. Although it's easy to say that a bourbon has vanilla or caramel, the real question is, what level or intensity of each flavor does the bourbon have? You don't need a complicated flavor wheel when choosing bourbons for your party; you can just plot your test run of tastings on an intensity chart (see the sample provided). This will help you identify how you want to use balance, counterbalance, and explosion for pairing a full dinner or an appetizer with multiple ingredients. Fruits, for example, have different intensities. If you taste apple in a bourbon, is it a golden, green, or Red Delicious apple? Each has a different level of apple flavor intensity. Sugar also has many variations—from pure cane sugar to brown sugar (light and dark) all the way to rich molasses and sorghum. What intensity do you note when you taste each bourbon?

After the intensity chart is complete, analyze the overall profile. Does it fall into the light or heavy flavor side or somewhere in between? Now taste the food you have selected. Is it heavy, light, or medium? Do you want to dial it up or down? Remember that bourbon pairings are about synergy and harmony.

If you are following a recipe, check the list of ingredients and mark them on the intensity chart to identify their flavors; then do the same with the bourbons. Soon, you won't even need the intensity chart, as you'll be a pro at recognizing the flavor intensity of many types of foods. You are creating your culinary vocabulary, just as you created your

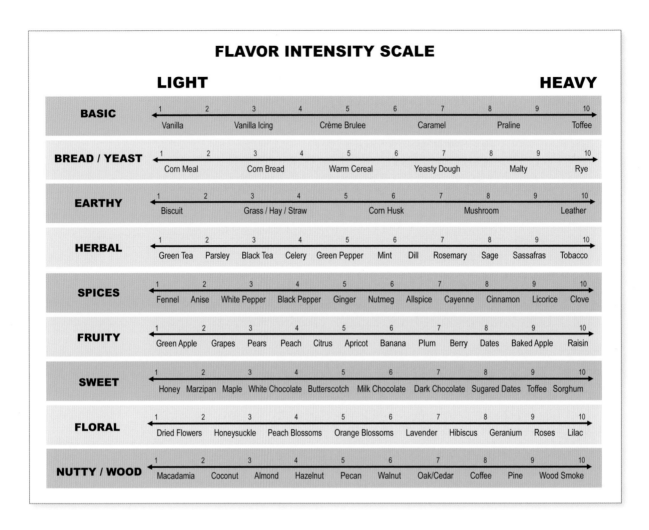

FLAVOR INTENSITY SCALE

LIGHT   **HEAVY**

	1	2	3	4	5	6	7	8	9	10
BASIC	Vanilla		Vanilla Icing		Crème Brulee		Caramel	Praline		Toffee
BREAD / YEAST	Corn Meal		Corn Bread		Warm Cereal		Yeasty Dough		Malty	Rye
EARTHY	Biscuit		Grass / Hay / Straw			Corn Husk		Mushroom		Leather
HERBAL	Green Tea	Parsley	Black Tea	Celery	Green Pepper	Mint	Dill	Rosemary	Sage	Sassafras · Tobacco
SPICES	Fennel · Anise	White Pepper	Black Pepper	Ginger	Nutmeg	Allspice	Cayenne	Cinnamon	Licorice	Clove
FRUITY	Green Apple	Grapes	Pears	Peach	Citrus · Apricot	Banana	Plum	Berry	Dates · Baked Apple	Raisin
SWEET	Honey · Marzipan	Maple	White Chocolate	Butterscotch	Milk Chocolate		Dark Chocolate	Sugared Dates	Toffee · Sorghum	
FLORAL	Dried Flowers	Honeysuckle	Peach Blossoms		Orange Blossoms		Lavender	Hibiscus · Geranium	Roses	Lilac
NUTTY / WOOD	Macadamia	Coconut	Almond	Hazelnut	Pecan	Walnut	Oak/Cedar	Coffee	Pine	Wood Smoke

bourbon vocabulary in chapter 3. Listed below are some quick hints for pairings.

SEQUENCE. Depending on the number of courses in your meal, go from a lighter bourbon to a heavier one for each course, in terms of both texture and proof. You don't want to overpower your guests too soon and deaden their palates.

SAUCES. Red sauces with a nice acidity hold up to higher-intensity grain-flavored bourbons. Cream sauces are best served with medium-intensity sweet and grainy bourbons. Overly intense smoky and earthy bourbons can overpower a sauce.

VINEGARY MARINADES. Marinades consisting of balsamic and other vinegars and warm spices are best served with sweeter bourbon profiles to tame the astringency.

VEGETABLES. Earthy and herbaceous wood-heavy bourbons impart a grilled effect to vegetables.

FRUITS. Almost all bourbons display fruity notes, so pairing the fruit you serve with a bourbon that has the same flavor profile is ideal. But decide whether you want to dial up a faint fruit note or balance a key flavor.

CHEESE. The intensity of the cheese plays a role. For example, pair goat cheese with a lighter bourbon such as Maker's Mark, and blue cheese with a heavier bourbon such as Baker's.

BEEF. Choose a bourbon with savory and bold flavors that stand up to the meat.

CHICKEN. Chicken is earthy and light, so pair it with a bourbon that is not too heavy or too high proof.

SEAFOOD. Lighter, softer, wheated whiskeys are a good choice with seafood.

SPICY AND PEPPERY FOODS. With spicy Asian and Hispanic food, serve heavily sweet bourbons.

SWEETS. Taste the bourbon for notes of milk chocolate or dark chocolate (it makes a difference), along with other descriptors such as caramel intensity and brown sugar. This will lead you to the right pairing of sweet food and bourbon.

The Cocktails

When you go to the liquor store to pick up mixers, bitters, and syrups for your cocktails, don't just choose whatever is on sale or a brand you know. When hosting an advanced pairing, selecting the accompaniments to bourbon is critical because these are indeed food flavors. Use a tasting mat to set up your pairings (see the sample provided).

Have you ever noticed that a certain bourbon tastes better in a Manhattan than in an old-fashioned? Or do you like a barrel-proof bourbon on the rocks but not in your cocktail? This is because of the structure and how the "weight" and flavors of the bourbon interact with the other cocktail ingredients. If I lined up three types of whiskey sour mix to make my cocktail, each would have its own flavor profile. One might be sweeter and heavier than another, so I would have to determine how that influenced my bourbon of choice. Mixologists are masters at doing this. They work with so many brands that they develop a

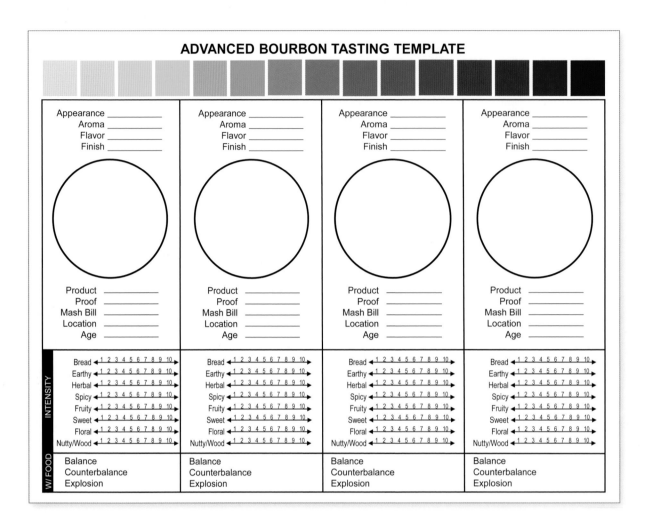

PARTY TRICK— Infuse your favorite fruit with a bourbon of like flavors and allow it to steep for a few days. You can add a complementary herb for a unique, ready-to-drink cocktail that is sure to be a crowd-pleaser.

kind of muscle memory of taste, so they can make choices quickly. They are truly bar chefs. And it's no accident that some mixologists make their own fresh-squeezed juices, syrups, and bitters. They want to control the freshness and brightness of the flavors when making cocktails.

The Dinner

You are ready to create your menu: what will you serve for dinner, and which bourbons will you pair with the various courses? Use the intensity chart described earlier to determine the right bourbon to serve with the meal. Three sample menu cards are illustrated here, one of which we designed for a Bourbon Women dinner with famed chef Susan Hershberg of Wiltshire Pantry. Note that on the menu cards, the bourbon is listed directly beneath the course. This is a helpful guide for your guests as you explain what they are tasting during each course.

Bourbon pineapple infusion for a crowd

Sample bottles for guests to take home

Rosemary chicken with gifts of potted rosemary

BOURBON • WOMEN

AMUSE-BOUCHE
Duck Confit Crepe Roulade
Herb Roulade filled with Duck Confit, Dark Cherry
Compote, Aged Balsamic Drizzle and
Topped with Crispy Shallot Wisps
Paired with Michter's Single Barrel Straight KY Rye

SUMMER BUFFET
Heirloom Tomato and Watermelon Salad
Local Feta, Arugula and Cilantro Mint Vinaigrette

Pan Seared All Natural Chicken Breast with Crispy Capers
Local Honey Bourbon Lemon Glaze and Shaved Parmesan

Grilled Asparagus with Pancetta-Hazelnut Relish

Roasted Heirloom Potatoes with Caramelized Onions

Sweet Kentucky Corn Pudding

DESSERT
Mini Red Velvet Whoopie Pies, Chocolate Pecan Bars,
and Coconut Petits Fours with Meringue Frosting
and Toasted Coconut

Assorted Bourbons

Aged to Perfection
BOURBON DINNER

MENU

Chopped Salad with Peanut-Citrus Dressing
Basil Hayden's

Asian Beef Tenderloin with Bourbon Glaze
Woodford Reserve

Served with Cheese Grits and
Bourbon Marinated Asparagus

Peppermint Dark Chocolate Lava Cake
Bakers

DRAM GOOD
BOURBON DINNER

MENU

Pomegranate Salad with Goat Cheese
Wilderness Trail Bourbon

Bourbon Marinated Rosemary Chicken
Balcone True Blue Straight Corn Whiskey

Served with Corn Pudding and
Farm Style Green Beans

Bourbon Soaked Raspberry Trifle
Balotin Chocolate Whiskey

There are countless ways to present a bourbon-based dinner entrée or to incorporate bourbon in your other courses. We have outlined a few examples of how to create a balanced menu that is both functional and aesthetically pleasing. Create your own versions by focusing on the entrée and then using the other dishes and sides to complement the main course.

Even if you choose not to cook with bourbon, we have a unique way of infusing bourbon into the meal: provide your guests with pipettes that they can use to inject bourbon directly into the food or to accent it with a quick taste of whiskey.

Pipettes filled with bourbon to infuse into the food pairing

SIX

A Bourbon Cocktail Soirée

I always wake up at the crack of ice.
—Joe E. Lewis

THE WORDS *cocktail party* conjure images of sophisticated, elegantly dressed people circulating through a room while exchanging witticisms and interesting conversation. The rattle of ice and spirits in a shaker or mixing beaker, plus the clink of glasses raised in a toast, provides the perfect soundscape for conviviality. Happily, you and your guests need not don dinner jackets or little black dresses to enjoy a cocktail party. But of course, you certainly can if you like.

Whatever the dress code, the great advantage to hosting a cocktail party is that it's not a dinner party. You can offer drinks, good conversation, and a bounty of small bites, and then, after an hour or two (with luck), everyone will head off to have dinner elsewhere. And you can relax and bask in the glow of knowing that they had a lovely time before you sent them on their merry way.

But before we launch into the nuts and bolts of the cocktail party, let's address the cocktail's creation. Like the beginnings of bourbon itself, that history is, shall we say, somewhat muddled.

What Exactly Is a Cocktail?

Essentially, a cocktail is a drink made with an alcoholic beverage combined with other ingredients. These can be other alcohols (such as the gin and vermouth in a martini), fruit juice, cream, or herbal infusions such as bitters. The main idea is the mixing and mingling of ingredients.

There are several stories about the origin of the word *cocktail*. Some are more plausible than others, but all are entertaining and can make for a lively topic of conversation at your party. Two are particularly colorful.

According to the first, the term originated in colonial America, the country most closely associated with cocktails. On one occasion, an eighteenth-century upstate New York tavern owner couldn't find a clean spoon and used the shaft of a rooster's (cock's) tail feather to stir drinks. The obvious question: why did he have a better supply of feathers than spoons? As we said, it's a colorful explanation.

The other is a bit more convoluted and is put forth pretty convincingly by award-winning drinks writer and scholar David Wondrich. The short

Preparing an old-fashioned station

version is that a London newspaper from 1798 mentioned a mixed drink of "a cocktail, vulgarly called ginger." The vulgarity apparently referred to a practice among horse dealers in Britain. According to Wondrich, when trying to sell an older, less than energetic steed, they would put "a clove of ginger up the poor tired creature's 'fundament' before showing it. This was done 'to make him lively and carry his tail [up].'" In other words, the horse's tail was cocked. Thus, the mixing of spirits with ginger (and other ingredients) became a "cocked tail" or "cocktail."

As Kentuckians, we share our state with a large population of equines, so we rather favor the second story. And for the record, as horse lovers, we disavow the ginger technique. But if you serve a Kentucky mule at your party (a variation of a Moscow mule made with bourbon and ginger beer), that would be a great time to tell the story.

Cocktail Party Food

The possibilities for cocktail party finger food are almost endless—emphasis on *finger*. If we had three hands instead of two, we would have no problem milling around a room with a plate in one hand, a drink in the second hand, and hand number three to transfer bites from plate to mouth. But we don't.

Of course, if there are clusters of seats where small groups can sit and talk and rest their drinks and plates on tables, that's great. You can also place bowls on those tables containing tidbits that can be eaten by hand (nuts, popcorn) or speared with a toothpick. Provide a little dish next to the tray of skewered hors d'oeuvres where people can discard their used toothpicks.

When deciding on the menu, keep in mind this very important suggestion: no gooey, flaky, or drippy foods. No one wants to mix and mingle with sticky fingers. Also, make sure that each finger food can be finished in no more than two or three bites.

PARTY TRICK—Who doesn't love Goldfish crackers? When Peggy was president of the Kentucky chapter of the American Institute of Wine & Food, she had the honor of taking Julia Child on a distillery tour and discovered that the cooking legend's favorite cocktail snack was Goldfish. These little crackers, which come in a variety of flavors, are great cocktail party snacks. Pretzel Goldfish offer a salty contrast to bourbon cocktails and can clear the palate.

Collection of serving-size plates for a cocktail party

PARTY TRICK—Use small plates. People tend to fill their plates at buffets, so keep the plates small. After all, this is not a dinner party, and small plates are easier to carry and perch on tables. You can choose festive paper plates that fit the theme of your party, bone china bread and butter plates, or something in between. The actual size should be six to seven inches in diameter.

Small bites

Another great finger food is the small sandwich. The bread helps absorb alcohol, and the options are almost endless. Three-inch dolly buns, available at bakeries and groceries, can hold a variety of fillings from sliced meats (roast beef, ham, and turkey are standards) and cheeses to savory spreads. Make sure you have enough variety so that everyone can find an appealing nibble, even guests who are vegetarians or who have dietary restrictions or food allergies. You can certainly save a great deal of time and energy by purchasing sandwich spreads from your favorite deli, but if you want to make your own, here are three recipes. Each makes enough for about 12 sandwiches using small buns.

Decorative bar carts are ideal for serving appetizers

∽ Pimento Cheese Spread

Makes about 1 cup

Known as the "caviar of the South," this spread can also be served on crackers of your choice.

    5 ounces grated sharp cheddar cheese
    ¼ cup finely chopped green olives
    ⅛ cup minced pimentos
    ¼ cup mayonnaise
    Dash of Worcestershire sauce

Combine all the ingredients in a food processer and chop briefly to blend. Refrigerate until ready to use. (Adapted from Charles Patterson's *Kentucky Cooking*.)

∽ Susan's Tuna Spread

Makes about 1 cup

Susan came across this recipe forty years ago in a small spiral-bound book of recipes by James Beard that was included with her purchase of a Cuisinart food processor. She always gets raves when she serves it. Spicy and tangy, this is not your bachelor uncle's bland tuna fish salad.

    2 5-ounce cans albacore tuna packed in water, drained
    ⅓ cup mayonnaise
    ¼ cup tightly packed fresh parsley sprigs
    Juice of 1 lemon
    1½ tablespoons coarsely ground black pepper

Combine all the ingredients in a food processor and blend briefly. Be careful not to let the spread get soupy. Chill before using.

⌒◦ *Benedictine*

Makes about 1 cup

Benedictine (not to be confused with the famous French liqueur) was the creation of early-twentieth-century Louisville caterer Jennie Benedict, author of *The Blue Ribbon Cookbook*. We can almost guarantee that you will not encounter Benedictine outside of Kentucky (and it is seldom found outside of Louisville). This particular recipe comes from award-winning cookbook writer and native Kentuckian Ronnie Lundy.

   3 tablespoons cucumber juice
   1 tablespoon onion juice
   8 ounces cream cheese, softened
   1 teaspoon salt
   A few grains cayenne pepper
   2 drops green food coloring

To obtain the juice, peel and grate a cucumber, wrap it in a clean dish towel, and squeeze the juice into a bowl. Discard the pulp. Do the same with the onion. Mix all the ingredients with a fork until well blended. Do not use a blender; it will make the spread too runny.

The Classic Drinks

The two classic bourbon cocktails are the old-fashioned and the Manhattan. But even though they are classic, there is no consensus on how to make them. The question of whether to muddle the fruit (and even which fruit to use) is the central debate surrounding the old-fashioned. And do you add water or soda to the drink? Preferences regarding the proportion of bourbon to vermouth in the Manhattan vary from one drinker to the next. And the amount of bitters can easily be overdone.

⌒◦ *Old-Fashioned*

   ½ ounce simple syrup (or 1 sugar cube)
   1 orange slice
   1 cherry
   3 dashes Angostura bitters
   1 ounce water
   2 ounces bourbon

Old-fashioned flare with a decorative tray and gold-rimmed vintage glassware

Put the syrup, orange, cherry, and bitters in an old-fashioned glass (also called a rocks glass). Gently press the fruit with a muddler to release some of the juices, but don't pulverize it. You don't want any unsightly clumps of fruit floating around in your drink.

If you used a sugar cube rather than syrup, add the water now, and use the muddler to crush it. (Sugar doesn't dissolve in alcohol.) Add the bourbon and the water if you used simple syrup. Fill the glass with ice and give it a good stir.

Some people leave out the cherry and use an orange peel instead of a slice. If you like the orange note, substitute orange bitters for the Angostura. If you like the cherry flavor, add a dash of cherry bitters. If you're feeling adventurous, add a dash of each. Feel free to experiment.

PARTY TRICK—Stock your do-it-yourself old-fashioned bar with fruits that are presliced and ready to drop in the glass. Perhaps gently muddle a blackberry, a strawberry, or a chunk of fresh pineapple or peach.

PARTY TRICK—If you have set up the bar so that guests can make their own old-fashioneds, provide sugar cubes soaked in bitters. In effect, you have already measured the bitters for them, saving a step. For a colorful presentation, use a variety of flavored bitters.

PARTY TRICK—To make old-fashioneds for ten guests, do it the easy way: before the party, combine 2½ cups of bourbon with 5 ounces of simple syrup, 10 ounces of water, and 2 tablespoons of bitters in a pitcher. Line up the glasses and add fruit to each. When you're ready to serve, give the fruit a quick press with the muddler (or not, for those of you in the anti-muddle camp), fill the glasses with ice, and pour in the premixed cocktail.

Interactive fruit-flavored old-fashioned station with labeled samples

If you're having a fairly large gathering, you may want to hire a bartender or a mixologist. What's the difference between the two? Generally, a bartender simply assembles drinks. A mixologist creates drinks, often his or her original creations or variations on the classics. As part of the entertainment, the bartender or mixologist can demonstrate how to make a cocktail or even lead your guests in mixing their own.

According to Kentucky legend, the old-fashioned was invented at Louisville's private Pendennis Club. Unfortunately, there is ample documentation that the drink appeared elsewhere before its supposed origin at the club. Nevertheless, the old-fashioned has been designated Louisville's official cocktail. Don't you wish you lived in a city with an official cocktail?

Of course, the Manhattan is identified with New York City. Interestingly, before Prohibition, each of New York's other boroughs had an eponymous cocktail too. The Brooklyn was made with whiskey, dry vermouth, and cherry liqueur. Gin was the spirit in both the Bronx and the Queens, while rum was used in the Staten Island.

The reasons the Manhattan survived should be pretty obvious. First, it's a great drink. Second, try to imagine a sophisticated cocktail enthusiast saying out loud in a bar, "Give me a Bronx, please." (No disrespect to the good people of the Bronx.)

PARTY TRICK—
Chill cocktail glasses
before adding the
beverage. Either store
them in the refrigerator
(if you have space) or
put ice in the glasses for
a few minutes and then
discard that ice before
pouring the drink.

PARTY TRICK—
Prepare all fruit garnish
prior to the party and
store in ziplock bags at
room temperature to
hold the juice.

Manhattan

3 ounces bourbon
1 ounce sweet vermouth
2 dashes Angostura bitters
1 stemmed cherry for garnish

Combine the bourbon, vermouth, and bitters in a mixing beaker with ice and stir until well chilled. Strain into a chilled, stemmed cocktail glass or coupe glass. Garnish with the cherry.

The proportions of each ingredient can be altered based on individual taste. Some recipes call for 2½ ounces of bourbon to 1½ ounces of vermouth. Some call for more bitters. (But beware: bitters are called bitters for good reason, and they can overwhelm a drink.) This is the recipe Susan uses for Manhattans, and Peggy loves Susan's Manhattans, so we are standing by this one. Obviously, you can experiment with the ingredients until you achieve the perfect Manhattan for you.

Upscale display for a Manhattan station

Incorporate decorative items between chocolate tasting cups with Luxardo cherries

Elevate glassware on tiered stands

PARTY TRICK—Elevate cocktails on stands to free up table space.

Whatever recipe you settle on, it's very easy to batch Manhattans ahead of time. Just multiply the ingredients by the number of drinks you want to serve and mix them in a pitcher with ice. Remove the ice and pop the pitcher in the refrigerator until party time.

You can also offer a flight of 1-ounce Manhattans made with three different bourbons and find out which one your guests prefer. (It's perfectly all right to use Glencairn glasses in place of cocktail glasses.) Bourbons with a higher rye content in their mash bills make a spicier Manhattan. Wheated bourbons may be smoother.

Whatever other bourbon choices you make, absolutely avoid high-proof, barrel-strength bourbon for cocktails. You want your guests to enjoy themselves and enjoy the flavors but *not* to overindulge.

The Mocktail

We cannot emphasize it enough: *responsible* drinking is important. You have probably noted that we favor quality over quantity. Some of your guests may choose not to drink or perhaps cannot drink alcohol for medical reasons. Of course, you still want them to have a good time and feel included in the fun. Enter mocktails—nonalcoholic drinks that offer a sophisticated alternative to a glass of ginger ale or sparkling water. Many bars are now adding them to their menus. There's also an organization, the Mocktail Project, that creates recipes; visit its website at https://themocktailproject.com.

⤳ *Kentucky Gent*

Although this drink looks bourbony, it isn't. It's both alcohol free and delicious.

> 3 ounces fresh grapefruit juice
> 1 ounce Gent's Original Spiced Blood Orange Cocktail Mix
> ½ ounce fresh lemon juice
> Ale-8-One (or ginger ale)
> Orange peel for garnish

Shake all the cocktail ingredients *except* the Ale-8-One over ice and strain into a cocktail glass. Top off with the Ale-8-One. Garnish with a twist of orange peel.

Music

If you are hosting a large party and space allows, you may want to hire musicians to play some mood music. (This works particularly well outdoors.) Although this can add to the festive mood, please be conscious of volume. You don't want your guests to have to shout at one another to be heard over the band.

The genre of music (pop, jazz, classical, bluegrass) depends on your taste, but acoustic rather than amplified music is preferable. It's intended to add to the ambience. It's not meant to be a performance.

Likewise, if you are using recorded music, keep the volume reasonable. The music should always be secondary to conversation.

By the Numbers

These measurements will help you plan quantities of spirits, ice, and other items you'll need for a party.

750 mL bottle of bourbon	= ~23 1-ounce pours
1 L bottle	= ~33 1-ounce pours
1.75 L bottle	= ~57 1-ounce pours
Ice	1½–2 pounds per person
Cocktail napkins	5 per guest
Drinks	2 drinks per person for the first hour 1 drink for the second hour
Bar (if using a bartender)	1 bar for up to 50 guests

When the party is over, we always do a bit of an inventory to determine how much product we used and which cocktails were more popular than others, so we can plan even more carefully for the next party.

PARTY TRICK—Give sealed containers of sample-sized cocktails to departing guests as party favors.

More Cocktail Recipes

This is primarily an entertaining guide, not a cookbook, but here are a few more cocktail recipes. See the appendix for recommended cookbooks (including those from which we've borrowed recipes) for additional help in populating your party tables.

ᕦ Kentucky Mule

Traditionally served in a copper mug, the Moscow mule is a drink made with vodka and ginger beer. In the past few years, scores of bars have started serving a bourbon version, and distillery gift shops are selling copper mugs. This recipe comes from *The Bourbon Bartender* by Jane Danger and Alla Lapushchik.

2 ounces bourbon
¾ ounce ginger beer
¾ ounce lime juice
Club soda
Candied ginger or lime for garnish

Combine the cocktail ingredients in a mule mug, stir, add ice, and garnish.

We asked Heather Wibbels, our friend and sister member of Bourbon Women, to provide some of her original cocktails for this book. She enthusiastically responded with the following recipes, with instructions for making both individual and batched cocktails. Heather won the Bourbon Women Association's annual Not-Your-Pink-Drink cocktail contest three years in a row. She is now the lead judge for the contest and has earned the title the Cocktail Contessa. You can find even more of her recipes on her website: https://www.cocktailcontessa.com.

⌒ Fleur-de-Lis Manhattan

Bourbon, chocolate, and raspberry combine in this classy cocktail to show your guests that bourbon can be paired with other spirits as well as food. Using Ballotin Bourbon Ball Whiskey adds both chocolate and pecan notes to the cocktail. Putting a bourbon ball (or an Art Eatables bourbon truffle) on a skewer for garnish is just icing on the cake. This sweet cocktail makes bourbon approachable for new enthusiasts, but it still has that smooth bourbon taste underneath the sweetness.

1½ ounces 100-proof bourbon
¾ ounce Ballotin Bourbon Ball Whiskey
¾ ounce Chambord liqueur
2 drops cardamom bitters
2 dashes chocolate bitters
Grated chocolate or bourbon ball for garnish

Combine the cocktail ingredients in a mixing glass filled with ice. Stir well and strain into a chilled martini glass or coupe glass. Add garnish.

⌒ Batched Fleur-de-Lis Manhattan

Serves 8 to 10

1½ cups 100-proof bourbon
¾ cup Ballotin Bourbon Ball Whiskey
¾ cup Chambord liqueur
16 drops cardamom bitters
16 dashes chocolate bitters
½ to ¾ cup water
Grated chocolate or bourbon ball for garnish

Combine the cocktail ingredients in a large pitcher or empty 750 mL bottle and mix well. Chill for several hours in the refrigerator. Before serving, chill for at least 30 minutes in the freezer. If guests will be pouring their own cocktails, place the bottle in an ice bucket to keep it cold while the party continues. Serve in a coupe glass or martini glass, and garnish with a bourbon ball or grated chocolate.

Dark Side

The Manhattan is a whiskey classic, but that classic can be darkened with the addition of some amaro, an Italian digestif. Amaro is bitter by nature, so a little goes a long way in a drink. Pair the amaro with some autumn bitters, such as Woodford's sorghum and sassafras bitters and some tiki bitters, and you've got a lovely dark drink, perfect for the fall.

2 ounces bourbon or rye whiskey (95 to 110 proof)
¼ ounce Carpano Antica sweet vermouth
¾ ounce Averna Amaro
8 drops Woodford's sorghum and sassafras bitters
4 drops Bittermans Elamakule Tiki bitters
Lemon peel and cocktail cherry for garnish

Combine all the cocktail ingredients in a mixing glass and fill with ice. Stir until well chilled, and strain into a chilled coupe glass or martini glass. Garnish with a high-quality cocktail cherry or two and a lemon peel that has been expressed over the cocktail.

Batched Dark Side

Serves 8 to 10

2 cups bourbon
¼ cup Carpano Antica sweet vermouth
¾ cup Averna Amaro
64 drops Woodford's sorghum and sassafras bitters (or to taste)
32 drops Bittermans Elamakule Tiki bitters (or to taste)
½ to ¾ cup water
Lemon peel and cocktail cherries for garnish

Combine all the cocktail ingredients in a large container and stir until well mixed. Chill in the refrigerator for several hours or overnight. Before serving, place in the freezer until well chilled. If guests will be pouring their own drinks, keep the container in an ice bucket so that it stays chilled throughout the party. Have lemon peel and cocktail cherries available for garnish.

～ Bold Old

The Bold Old is based on a traditional old-fashioned recipe, but the heat makes it a little more aggressive. It starts with a high-proof spirit and adds smoky, spicy bitters for some heat. The smoke is reminiscent of how it smells on the cooperage floor near the barrel-charring stations. It's smoky, but not overwhelming. The bitters also bring some heat to the cocktail. In the same way that cayenne is used in Mexican hot chocolate, the bitters increase the sensation of heat and extend the finish without adding a lot of other flavors, allowing the whiskey to be the star. Charring activates the oils in the cinnamon stick and accentuates the smoke in the bitters, tying the drink together.

2 ounces Old Forester Whiskey Row 1920 (115 proof)
  or any high-proof bourbon (at least 110 proof)
½ ounce demerara syrup (1:1 ratio of demerara sugar to water)
3 to 4 dashes Hella Bitters Smoked Chili bitters
Charred cinnamon stick for garnish

Combine the cocktail ingredients in a mixing glass and fill with ice. Stir and strain into a rocks glass with fresh ice. Garnish with the charred cinnamon stick.

～ Batched Bold Old

Serves 8 to 10

2 cups Old Forester Whiskey Row 1920
½ cup demerara simple syrup (1:1 ratio of demerara sugar to water)
24 to 32 dashes Hella Bitters Smoked Chili bitters
½ cup water
Charred cinnamon sticks for garnish

Combine the cocktail ingredients in an empty 750 mL bottle and mix well. It's easiest to add the bitters (start with the lower number of dashes) to the simple syrup before adding it to the bottle. Chill the bottle well in the refrigerator. Once it is chilled, do a taste test and add more bitters as needed. Make sure the drink is completely chilled before serving in rocks glasses over ice. Garnish with a charred cinnamon stick.

∽ Kentucky Promise

This cocktail recipe was created as a wedding gift for friends. It's close to an old-fashioned but a little sweeter. To balance the strong blackberry sweetness that comes from the whiskey and the syrup, the Averna Amaro acts as a bittering agent. The Kentucky Promise can be served neat or on the rocks.

1½ ounces Angel's Envy Bourbon
1 ounce Starlight Blackberry Whiskey
½ ounce Averna Amaro
½ ounce blackberry simple syrup (see below)
Fresh blackberry, mint, or basil leaf for garnish

Combine the cocktail ingredients in a mixing glass and fill with ice. Stir until well chilled and strain into an ice-filled (or not) old-fashioned glass. Add garnish.

BLACKBERRY SIMPLE SYRUP
1 cup sugar
3 cups frozen blackberries
¼ cup water

Combine the ingredients in a saucepan and cook until the blackberries are thawed, soft, and very juicy. Once it starts to boil, reduce the heat and simmer for 10 minutes. Strain the blackberries out, pressing on them to extract as much juice as possible. Let the syrup cool. It can be stored in a bottle for one to two weeks.

The proper way to hold a plate and cocktail: Place your napkin under the plate, supported by your fingers, and rest the glass on top of the plate, secured by your thumb. Your other hand is free to eat and shake hands!

⌒ Batched Kentucky Promise

Serves 8 to 10

> 1½ cups Angel's Envy Bourbon
> 1 cup Starlight Blackberry Whiskey
> ½ cup Averna Amaro
> ½ cup blackberry simple syrup (see above)
> ½ to ¾ cup water
> Fresh blackberry, mint, or basil leaf for garnish

Combine all the cocktail ingredients in a large container and stir until well mixed. Chill for at least several hours or overnight in the refrigerator. Place the container in the freezer for 30 minutes just before serving, and keep it in an ice bucket if guests will be serving themselves to ensure that it stays chilled throughout the party. The Kentucky Promise can be served either neat in a coupe glass or a martini glass or over ice in a rocks glass. If serving in a coupe or martini glass, use a single spanked mint or basil leaf as garnish. If serving in a rocks glass over ice, a small sprig of mint or basil dresses it up nicely. Note: To "spank" mint or other herbs, lay the leaf in the palm of one hand and slap it with the other. This releases the aromatic oils.

⌒ Apple Pie Old-Fashioned

The flavors of fall abound in this cocktail, which uses apple brandy and maple syrup to sweeten the old-fashioned. A tiny bit of cinnamon whiskey adds a hint of pie spice.

> 1½ ounces bourbon (90 to 100 proof)
> 1 ounce Copper & Kings Apple Brandy (or any apple brandy)
> ¼ ounce maple syrup
> 1 bar spoon cinnamon whiskey (Evan Williams preferred)
> ½ dropper Bittermans Elamakule Tiki bitters
> Dash of fresh nutmeg, apple slice, and/or cinnamon stick for garnish

Combine the cocktail ingredients in a mixing glass. Add ice and stir until well chilled. Strain into a rocks glass with ice and add garnish.

⌐ Batched Apple Pie Old-Fashioned

Serves 4

 1½ cups bourbon
 1 cup Copper & Kings Apple Brandy (or any apple brandy)
 ¼ cup maple syrup
 1½ ounces cinnamon whiskey (Evan Williams preferred)
 ¾ cup water
 20 drops Bittermans Elamakule Tiki bitters
 Dash of nutmeg, apple slices, and/or cinnamon sticks for garnish

Combine the ingredients in a pitcher or container that holds at least 32 ounces. Stir to mix. Refrigerate until well chilled. If you'll be serving this in the pitcher, add some cinnamon sticks and apple slices to dress it up. For individual servings, pour into a rocks glass with ice and garnish with an apple slice, cinnamon stick, or both.

⟡ Porch Swing

June evenings are perfect for sitting out on the deck and enjoying the weather. Take a break from your evening plans and indulge in this low-proof, easy-to-make cocktail. Or if you need a cocktail to sip while preparing dinner or presiding over the grill, this one has you covered. Adding the lavender bitters just before serving spices up the cocktail in a lovely floral way.

> 1½ ounces bourbon
> 2 ounces fresh orange juice
> 4 ounces fresh lemonade
> Sparkling water
> 3 drops lavender bitters (optional)
> Orange or lemon wheel for garnish

Add the bourbon, orange juice, and lemonade to a highball glass or Collins glass filled with ice. Stir once or twice with a bar spoon to incorporate the ingredients, and top with a splash of sparkling water. Just before serving, add the lavender bitters—it takes the cocktail from tasty to wow! Garnish with an orange or lemon wheel.

⟡ Batched Porch Swing

Serves 8 to 10

> 1½ cups bourbon
> 2 cups orange juice
> 4 cups lemonade
> 30 drops lavender bitters
> 1 to 2 cups sparkling water
> Orange and lemon slices

Add the bourbon, orange juice, lemonade, and bitters to a container and mix well. Chill overnight or for several hours. Just before serving, add the sparkling water and some orange and lemon slices to the pitcher. Serve in Collins glasses filled with ice, and spritz a bit of lavender bitters on top of each drink. Garnish each with a lemon and orange slice.

Pretty as a Peach

Peach season is short, so take advantage of it because this drink wows everyone. It's perfect for a smaller gathering of friends, even though it requires a little more preparation than some other cocktails. Note: You can use frozen peaches, but they need to be completely defrosted so that they muddle correctly.

> 2 ounces 90-proof bourbon
> ½ lemon, peeled and quartered
> ½ peach, peeled and sliced
> 3 dashes Fee Brothers peach bitters
> 1 dash Fee Brothers gin-aged orange bitters
> 3 mint leaves
> 1 ounce simple syrup (1:1 ratio of sugar to water)
> 1 ounce water
> Fresh mint sprig and peach slice for garnish

Muddle everything except the bourbon and garnish. Then add the bourbon and some ice, shake, and strain into a rocks glass with ice. Class it up with a garnish of spanked mint and a peach slice. Voilà—the perfect summer drink!

Batched Pretty as a Peach

Serves 2 to 3

> 4 ounces 90-proof bourbon
> 1 lemon, peeled and quartered
> 1 peach, peeled and sliced
> 6 dashes Fee Brothers peach bitters
> 2 dashes Fee Brothers gin-aged orange bitters
> 6 mint leaves
> 2 ounces simple syrup (1:1 ratio of sugar to water)
> 2 ounces water
> Fresh mint sprigs and peach slices for garnish

Muddle everything except the bourbon and garnish. Then add the bourbon, fill with ice, shake until well chilled (at least in the 30s), and strain into rocks glasses with ice. Garnish with spanked mint and a peach slice.

Serves 8

 1 cup water
 1 cup sugar
 2 tablespoons minced fresh ginger
 2 very ripe peaches, halved, pitted, and thinly sliced
 2 liters seltzer, chilled
 16 fresh mint leaves for garnish

In a medium saucepan over medium-low heat, bring the water, sugar, and ginger to a gentle simmer, stirring to dissolve the sugar. Remove the simple syrup from the heat, cover, and steep for about 30 minutes. Over a medium bowl, pour the syrup through a fine-mesh sieve, pressing the ginger against the sieve with the back of a spoon to extract the flavor. Discard the ginger. Cover the bowl with plastic wrap and refrigerate until well chilled. Evenly distribute the peach slices among 8 tall glasses. Lightly press the peaches with the back of a wooden spoon to release their juice. Pour about 2 tablespoons of chilled syrup over the peaches. (Store the remaining syrup in the refrigerator for up to two weeks.) Add ice cubes; then top with seltzer. Stir to distribute the syrup, peach juice, and seltzer evenly. Garnish with 2 mint leaves.

The proper way to hold a cocktail plate and glass

SEVEN

The Kentucky Derby Party

*When everyone is a
Kentuckian for a day.
—Peggy*

KENTUCKY'S TWO SIGNATURE PRODUCTS are bourbon whiskey and Thoroughbred racehorses. This is not a coincidence. The state's abundant supply of limestone-filtered water is the key. Filled with calcium and magnesium, the water helps build strong bones in horses. It is also iron free, which is crucial for whiskey making. Water containing iron would turn bourbon black. So, thanks to this abundant water supply, Thoroughbreds and bourbon mature side by side in the Bluegrass.

Every spring, horses and whiskey meet to celebrate "the greatest two minutes in sports," the Kentucky Derby, which is run at Churchill Downs in Louisville on the first Saturday in May. The Derby is also called the Run for the Roses because the winner's neck is draped with a garland of red roses. While the race itself doesn't last very long, it has given rise to what we Kentuckians like to think of as the greatest two weeks in partying. Other places have four seasons, but Kentucky has five—summer, fall, winter, spring, and Derby.

During those two weeks of partying, restaurants host bourbon-themed dinners, often featuring the official drink of the Kentucky Derby: the mint julep (much more about that shortly). Bourbon flows freely at a series of galas held to raise money for a variety of charities. And the drinks aren't limited to juleps. Louisville has its own official bourbon cocktail: the old-fashioned. Residents entertain visitors from out of town who have come to attend the race or simply to enjoy the festivities.

Derby History

The first Kentucky Derby took place in 1875, which makes it the oldest continuously held sporting event in the United States. The winner that year was a chestnut colt named Aristides. After making a fortune in the California gold rush, his owner had returned to Kentucky and started a horse farm.

The winner of the 1914 Derby, Old Rosebud, had a solid bourbon pedigree. He was owned by H. C. Applegate, whose father served on the board of directors of Churchill Downs and owned a distillery that produced a bourbon called Rosebud. So that year's Derby winner

Decorative rose garland for your front door

was named after a bourbon brand, as was the 1920 winner Paul Jones. (Neither brand exists today, but the Jones family was responsible for another brand that is still around—Four Roses.)

And here's another bit of horse and whiskey trivia: the legendary Stitzel-Weller Distillery in Louisville, which was owned in part by Julian "Pappy" Van Winkle, opened on Derby Day 1935. The winner that year was Omaha, who went on to become one of only thirteen horses to win racing's coveted Triple Crown—the Kentucky Derby, the Preakness, and the Belmont Stakes.

An average of 160,000 people cram into Churchill Downs on Derby Day, which also features a phenomenon unique to American sporting events: People dress up. Fancy hats and colorful dresses are de rigueur for women. Men sport neckties featuring equine motifs and don brightly colored blazers and trousers they would never wear to the office.

Millions more celebrate at home and watch the race on television, which is broadcast nationally. Derby parties are held across the country, some of them hosted by homesick Kentuckians. This gives them a great excuse to stand and sing the state song, "My Old Kentucky Home," which is played just as the horses step onto the track. In fact, on Derby Day, everyone can be a Kentuckian.

Your Derby Day Party

Signal that yours is a Derby house by hanging a life-size horseshoe or a wreath of roses on the door. Plan activities for both inside and outside—volleyball, corn hole, and, for the kids, mock races with stick horses. As your guests arrive, distribute programs and tip sheets (you can find them online) with Derby apps for insider information. All that fun is sure to work up an appetite.

From formal affairs to casual in-home gatherings, signature Kentucky foods and beverages are traditional for Derby parties. They include country ham served on beaten biscuits or yeast buns, sliced beef tenderloin with Henry Bain's sauce, burgoo stew, Benedictine spread, corn pudding, cheese grits, tomato aspic, limestone Bibb lettuce salad, and assorted fruit and nut pies and cakes. Don't forget the nibbles, such as fine cashews or cheese straws. And in advance of your gathering, assemble all the mixers, simple syrups, garnishes, and ice—both crushed and block—you'll need.

For a casual in-home Derby party, encourage your guests to be both comfortable and festive when it comes to clothing. Zany hats, for instance, fit the energy of the track, and you can have a contest and award a prize for the best Derby hat.

PARTY TRICK— Print copies of the lyrics to "My Old Kentucky Home" and distribute them to your guests so they can sing along, too. You can find them at https://www.kentuckyderby.com.

PARTY TRICK— Purchase a few copies of the Daily Racing Form to have on hand for guests who are really serious about handicapping the race. Check with your local magazine dealer or bookstore a few weeks ahead of time to make sure copies will be available.

Just as race-goers place their bets at the track, there is traditionally a betting pool at home parties. Write the names of all the horses in the race on separate slips of paper, put them in a hat, and pass it around. Whatever horse each guest draws is the one he or she is rooting for. You can award prizes to the first-, second-, and third-place winners. The prizes can be cash that everyone has contributed to a pool ($1 per guest is fine, but you can up the ante if your guests are game). Of course, bottles of bourbon make nice prizes too. Other options include boxes of bourbon candy or other bourbon-infused foods, such as bottled sauces.

When guests are ready to leave, offer them a potted mint plant to grow in the backyard or bourbon candy wrapped in a faux julep cup. Miniature bottles of bourbon are always welcome parting gifts. On Derby Day, every drop of hospitality is offered to guests until their final departure.

The Official Drink

Mint juleps probably became a Derby tradition because mint grows abundantly in spring and summer, just in time for race parties. Bourbon, too, was abundant, but the quality of the whiskey of the 1800s wasn't

PARTY TRICK—
Try using mint-infused bourbon in your juleps. The following technique comes from renowned Lexington-area chef Ouita Michel, owner of the Holly Hill in Midway. Right after Derby Day, she fills an empty bourbon bottle with as much fresh mint as she can pack into it. She then pours bourbon into the bottle, seals it, and sets it in a cool, dark place for a year. Next Derby Day, she uses it in juleps.

Traditional mint julep

as good as it is today. The simple syrup used in the julep (two parts sugar to one part boiled water) helped make the drink palatable. The traditional silver julep cups trace their roots to horseracing trophies. The winners celebrated by drinking from them. The trophy cups held not only the beverage but also chipped ice obtained from a large block at the barn. The contents developed a cold, frosty layer that kept the sipper refreshed on a sweltering Kentucky day.

Your julep cups don't have to be silver. The official Churchill Downs julep glass is a collector's item. The track issues a different design each year with the names of all previous Derby winners listed on the side. You can purchase the current year's glasses online for your in-home party, and they are inexpensive enough that you can give them to your guests as keepsakes.

One thing Kentuckians agree to disagree about is how to make a mint julep and who makes the best version.

ᘯ *Mint Julep*

1 ounce simple syrup
3 to 5 fresh mint leaves, plus a fresh sprig for garnish
3 ounces Kentucky bourbon
Crushed ice

To make the simple syrup, add 2 cups of granulated sugar to 1 cup of boiling water. Cool, bottle, and refrigerate. You can do this the day before the party.

Derby glassware collection

To make the julep, place the simple syrup and mint leaves in the bottom of a julep cup or glass. Muddle. Add bourbon and stir. Fill to the brim with crushed ice, add a long straw, and garnish with a mint sprig. (Note: If you are using mint-infused bourbon, don't use the muddled mint leaves.)

JULEP VARIATIONS

You can substitute a variety of ingredients for the mint and make alterations to the syrups. Here are a few suggestions:

Pineapple Julep: Muddle a tablespoon of chopped fresh pineapple with mint leaves and use 2 ounces of bourbon and 1 ounce of pineapple juice.

Peach-Basil Julep: Use fresh basil leaves and a split vanilla bean to make the simple syrup and add 2 5½-ounce cans of peach nectar to the syrup. Muddle a peach slice instead of mint.

Strawberry Julep: Add 3 fresh chopped strawberries to the bottom of the glass, along with the mint and syrup, and muddle.

Chocolate Julep: No muddling needed here. Simply combine 2 ounces Kentucky bourbon, 1 ounce white crème de menthe, and 1 ounce dark crème de cacao; shake over ice; and pour into a stemmed cocktail glass. Garnish with a sprig of mint.

Flavored marmalade syrups

Other Cocktails

Of course, bourbon will be the main spirit for your Derby party. But we bourbon lovers can't be selfish. Bloody Marys, beer, and champagne are also celebratory concoctions. The Seelbach Cocktail is made with bourbon and champagne. It is the signature cocktail of Louisville's historic Seelbach Hotel, which was mentioned in *The Great Gatsby* and has been welcoming Derby guests since it opened in 1905.

⌐ Seelbach Cocktail

1½ ounces bourbon
1½ ounces Cointreau
7 dashes Angostura bitters
7 dashes Peychaud's bitters
Chilled brut champagne or California sparkling wine to top up
Orange twist for garnish

Pour each of the ingredients, in the order listed, into a champagne flute. Top off with champagne. Garnish with an orange twist.

You can make a dynamite Bloody Mary by substituting bourbon for vodka. (Come to think of it, when is it *not* a good idea to substitute bourbon for vodka?) The late Louisville mixologist Joy Perrine, who was a member of the Kentucky Bourbon Hall of Fame, created this recipe. Called the Dark and Bloody Bourbon Mary (supposedly, the indigenous people of what became Kentucky called the land the "dark and bloody ground"), it is reproduced here from the book she coauthored with Susan, *The Kentucky Bourbon Cocktail Book*. By the way, the only way to match the flavor of this recipe exactly is to use bourbon-smoked spices and barrel-aged Worcestershire sauce from Bourbon Barrel Foods (see the appendix).

⌒ Dark and Bloody Bourbon Mary

1 teaspoon salt, pepper, paprika mix
2 ounces bourbon
2 large lemon wedges
1 tablespoon Worcestershire sauce
1 can (6 ounces) tomato juice

To prepare the seasoning mix, combine in a mortar (or spice grinder) one part each smoked sea salt, smoked black pepper, and smoked paprika (all from Bourbon Barrel Foods). Finely crush with a pestle and shake together in a jar.

To a pint glass or a large mason jar filled with ice, add the bourbon, squeeze and drop in the lemon wedges, and add 1 teaspoon of the seasoning mix and the Worcestershire sauce. Shake. Add more ice and the tomato juice. Shake again. Garnish with a long straw and baby corn, large pitted black olive, and cherry pepper, all on a stick.

We served this to a crowd at the New Orleans Bourbon Festival by making a large batch ahead of time and refrigerating it. When it was time to serve, we poured the drinks into Glencairn glasses, each containing an ice cube and a black olive.

Bloody Mary

Corn pudding on the Derby buffet

The Buffet Table

"Table luxuries" is Kentucky-speak for Derby buffet tables with the finest culinary and seasonal delicacies. When planning the Derby menu and décor for your party, ask yourself: Elegant or casual? What time of day? Brunch, evening meal after the race, or all-day soirée? You can serve many of the same foods with *all* styles of entertaining, but the degree to which you dial up or down your table settings—china, crystal, and silverware—sets your party aesthetics.

Choose a bright tablecloth to represent the jockey silks. Native Kentucky botanicals such as forsythia, hydrangea, azalea, and, of course, roses make great centerpieces.

If you have silver trays, use them. They are traditional to Derby Day. You can mix in wooden pieces, baskets, and stoneware to vary the level of elegance. Use julep cups to hold the silverware, or roll the silverware in linen napkins tied with ribbons that match the tablecloth. For a down-home Kentucky touch, substitute rope twine for the ribbon. If you're using your finest china, have it on the buffet table, stacked and ready. For more casual settings, there are myriad Derby and horse-themed paper plates and napkins. This is also the perfect occasion to use the official Derby glasses. If you have the space, separate the dessert table from the buffet to showcase the desserts and the perfect bourbon pairings.

Ensemble of silver for an elegant Derby party

*Rose garnish and strawberries add color to
country ham and biscuits*

Formal Derby presentation

Casual Derby setting

Traditional Derby Buffet Foods: Casual versus Elegant

There is a lot of overlap in traditional Derby dishes because they are easy to upgrade from casual to elegant. The main difference in the two types of buffets is presentation: Silver trays for elegant, wooden or melamine for casual. China for elegant, stoneware or paper plates for casual. You get the idea. Here's a breakdown of menu items:

Elegant

Long-stem strawberries
Shrimp cocktail
Cheddar wafers
Country ham and beaten biscuits with bourbon marmalade
Benedictine tea sandwiches
Bibb lettuce with bourbon vinaigrette
Tomato aspic
Burgoo
Steamed asparagus with hard-boiled egg crumbles, red pepper
Fancy potatoes (fingerling, duchess, or lyonnaise)
Sliced beef tenderloin with Henry Bain's sauce
Corn pudding
Cheese grits
Homemade yeast rolls
Bourbon chocolate-dipped strawberries
Bourbon candy and truffles
Louisville chocolate chip pie

Casual

Strawberries
Country ham and biscuits with bourbon marmalade
Mixed green salad with Bibb lettuce
Burgoo
Pimento cheese and Benedictine spread
Barbecued ribs
Fried chicken
Cheese grits
Baked beans
Corn bread
Broccoli casserole
Louisville chocolate chip tartlets
Pecan pie
Bourbon candy

Burgoo is a stew that traces its origins to frontier Kentucky. It was a way to use game and whatever garden vegetables might be on hand. (We promise there's no squirrel or bear in any modern burgoo.) It was also easy to prepare in very large quantities, and some recipes made up to 150 servings! (Yes, that would require a very large kettle.) There are so many versions of burgoo that entire cookbooks have been written on the subject (see the appendix). The following recipe is from our friend Albert Schmid's *Burgoo, Barbecue & Bourbon*.

⌒ *Delicious Burgoo*

Serves 10

3 tablespoons bacon fat
1 pound beef stew meat
1 chicken, quartered
2 quarts water
2 teaspoons salt
1½ cups onions, chopped
1 clove garlic, minced
1 cup potatoes, diced
4 stalks celery, diced
1 can (19 ounces) tomatoes
3 carrots, diced
1 cup green pepper, chopped
8 to 10 ounces frozen lima beans
⅛ teaspoon crushed red pepper
1 bay leaf
2 teaspoons brown sugar
¼ teaspoon black pepper
1 cup okra, sliced
8 ounces frozen corn
¼ cup butter
½ cup flour
¼ cup parsley, chopped

In a large Dutch oven, combine 2 tablespoons of the bacon fat and the beef. Brown the meat on all sides. Add the chicken, water, and salt. Cover and cook slowly over medium heat until the meat is tender. Remove the beef and chicken from the Dutch oven. Take the chicken off the bones and discard the bones. Cut the beef and chicken into large pieces and return them to the broth in the Dutch oven. In a frying pan, cook the onions in the remaining tablespoon of bacon fat until tender; add the onions to the broth. Add the garlic, potatoes, celery, tomatoes, carrots, green pepper, lima beans, red pepper, bay leaf, brown sugar, and black pepper. Cook slowly, stirring occasionally, for 2 hours. Add the okra and corn and cook for 15 minutes. In a bowl, combine the butter and flour; blend into the burgoo. Sprinkle with parsley before serving.

Because corn pudding and cheese grits are so iconic, we've provided recipes for both, which can serve as anchoring side dishes. They have the same base ingredient as bourbon—corn. The corn pudding recipe comes from our friend chef David Larson, who for many years had a wonderful restaurant in Lexington called the Pampered Chef. The grits recipe is generic. You'll find variations in many cookbooks.

⌒◯ *Corn Pudding*

Serve 8 to 10

4 cups fresh corn kernels (about 8 ears)
½ cup sugar
2 teaspoons flour
1 teaspoon salt
1½ teaspoons baking powder
6 eggs, beaten
2 cups heavy cream
1 cup half-and-half
2 tablespoons butter, melted

Preheat the oven to 350 degrees. Process 1 cup of corn in a food processor until it's ground. Combine the ground corn, the remaining 3 cups of corn kernels, sugar, flour, salt, and baking powder in a bowl and mix well. Whisk the eggs, heavy cream, and half-and-half in a bowl until blended and stir into the corn mixture. Add the butter and mix well.

Pour the mixture into a greased 9- by 13-inch baking pan and bake for 40 minutes, or until a sharp knife inserted in the center comes out clean. You can substitute frozen corn for fresh.

⤳ Cheese Grits

Serves 6 (simply multiply ingredients for a larger crowd)

½ cup stone-ground grits
¾ teaspoon salt
4 tablespoons (½ stick) butter
½ cup shredded sharp cheddar cheese
Cayenne pepper to taste (optional)
3 eggs, separated

Preheat the oven to 375 degrees. In a heavy saucepan, bring 2½ cups of salted water to a boil and add the grits. Simmer over medium heat, stirring constantly, for about 20 minutes. Stir in the butter and remove from the heat. Add the cheese, cayenne, and egg yolks. Cover and set aside. Beat the egg whites until stiff and stir them into the grits. Pour the mixture into a 1-quart buttered baking dish and bake 35 to 40 minutes until golden brown.

Given that Bibb is Kentucky's native lettuce, we have to include a Bibb lettuce salad. This one is adapted from *The Kentucky Bourbon Cookbook*, as is the Kentucky Chocolate Bourbon Pecan Pie recipe that follows.

⤳ Kentucky Bibb Salad with Bourbon Vinaigrette and Toasted Pecans

Serves 8

BIBB SALAD
2 cups toasted pecan halves
6 heads Bibb lettuce, washed and patted dry
24 heirloom tomatoes or 4 large tomatoes
24 red grape tomatoes
2 red onions, diced (optional)

Spread the pecans on a baking sheet and toast in a 350-degree oven for about 5 minutes. Set aside. Break the lettuce apart. Cut the small tomatoes in half and slice the large tomatoes. Add the lettuce, tomatoes, and red onions (if used) to a large salad bowl.

BOURBON VINAIGRETTE

½ cup cider vinegar

5 tablespoons bourbon

½ cup brown mustard

4 tablespoons honey

4 tablespoons barbecue sauce

3 teaspoons ground pepper

3 teaspoons garlic chili sauce

Mix all the dressing ingredients together, add to the salad bowl along with the toasted pecans, and toss.

Kentucky Chocolate Bourbon Pecan Pie

Serves 6

ALL-PURPOSE PASTRY

1½ cups all-purpose flour

½ teaspoon salt

1½ cups sugar

½ cup very cold unsalted butter cut into pieces

2 extra large egg yolks, lightly beaten

¼ cup ice water

To make the pastry, combine the flour, salt, and sugar in a mixing bowl. Cut the butter into the flour mixture using a pastry blender until the mixture resembles coarse meal. With your hands, gradually add the egg yolks and ice water until a ball of dough forms (do not overwork the dough). Wrap the dough in plastic and chill for 30 minutes. Roll the chilled dough out on a lightly floured surface into a circle 12 inches in diameter and about ⅛ inch thick. Place the dough in a 10-inch pie pan and preheat the oven to 375 degrees.

PIE FILLING

3 extra large eggs

1 cup sugar

2 tablespoons butter, melted

1 cup dark corn syrup

1 teaspoon vanilla extract

¼ cup bourbon

½ cup semisweet chocolate chips

1 cup pecan halves

To make the filling, beat the eggs, sugar, melted butter, corn syrup, vanilla, and bourbon in a mixing bowl. Strain this mixture into another bowl using a fine mesh. Sprinkle the chocolate chips on the bottom of the unbaked piecrust and cover with a layer of pecans. Pour the filling on top of the chocolate and pecans. Bake for 35 to 40 minutes. The pie is done when a knife inserted 2 inches from the side comes out clean. Cool for at least 30 minutes before serving.

Note: If you want to make individual tartlets, line the wells of a muffin pan with the pastry and add equal amounts of filling to each.

EIGHT

Bourbon Tables

HOW KENTUCKY DISTILLERIES ENTERTAIN

Bourbonism *is*
our 365-day-a-year
tourism industry.
—Greg Fischer,
mayor of Louisville

AS YOU'VE PROBABLY GATHERED BY NOW, bourbon has always been central to Kentucky culture. With a nationwide decline in the popularity of whiskey in the 1970s and 1980s, we Kentuckians pretty much had bourbon to ourselves. Then, about twenty years ago, interest in bourbon started to rise. Americans—and indeed, people around the world—discovered that bourbon was delicious, but the spirit was appealing on another important level. Consumers started to take an interest in where their food and drink came from and the quality of ingredients, and they were impressed that the production of bourbon could be traced to an identifiable place: 95 percent of bourbon comes from Kentucky. As a result, people wanted to see where bourbon was made.

The popularity of "bourbon tourism" came as a surprise to most distilleries. Even though other industries such as automobile makers and soft drink manufacturers had offered tours of their plants for years, it didn't occur to the heads of Kentucky distilleries that anyone would want to see where and how bourbon was made. The notable exception was Maker's Mark, which opened to visitors decades before any other distillery did so.

Oh my, how that has changed! Today, Kentucky's distilleries welcome nearly three million visitors a year. The experience has grown from a simple distillery tour that ended with a refreshing sip of iced tea—offering whiskey tastings was prohibited by state law—to a wide range of activities. Visitors' centers have been expanded into de facto museums with exhibits covering the history of the industry in general and of the distillery's brand in particular. The Kentucky Distillers' Association launched the Kentucky Bourbon Trail, which Peggy helped develop (https://kybourbontrail.com). Louisville has an Urban Bourbon Trail (https://www.bourboncountry.com) that features restaurants and bars with great bourbon selections. And many distilleries, both historic and new, have added culinary programs with resident chefs, cocktail bars, and events facilities. Almost all have full-time guest services and events managers.

Our distilleries are no longer just making bourbon; they are welcoming visitors with true Kentucky hospitality, and each has its own special style of entertaining. The following sampling of both small and large distilleries highlights their unique approach to greeting and accommodating guests and provides some of their best recipes. But they all exhibit their "best in show" when it comes to bourbon hospitality. Please visit their websites or give them a call for more details about their tours, bar hours, and upcoming culinary events.

The Bardstown Bourbon Company, Bardstown

https://www.bardstownbourbon.com
Bottle & Bond Kitchen and Bar, 502-252-6331

Bardstown Bourbon Company has brought a contemporary bourbon sensibility to Nelson County, the historic epicenter of bourbon making. As director of bourbon education, guest experience, and product development Dan Callaway explains, "We are a modern take on bourbon. But we want to show where bourbon came from." That ambition has resulted in a remarkable number of parts to Bardstown Bourbon Company (BBC).

Kentucky Hall of Fame distiller Steve Nally (formerly of Maker's Mark) heads the distillery itself. BBC not only makes its own whiskey but also "collaborates" with more than twenty other distilleries and brands to make whiskey. There are more than thirty different mash bills.

The site's restaurant, the Bottle & Bond Kitchen and Bar, is headed by chef Felix Mosso, formerly of the storied Green Briar Resort in West Virginia. The menu features traditional ingredients in new dishes such as sweet potato gnocchi (see the recipe below) and fried oysters and grits. You can even order a bourbon-laced milk shake for dessert: the Entrepreneur contains Bardstown Bourbon Company Collaboration Bourbon, malt chocolate, chocolate syrup, and chocolate-bar garnish.

The bar strives to carry every brand of bourbon made in Kentucky and has a staff of mixologists who not only create craft drinks but also teach cocktail classes. If that were not enough, there is a curated collection of more than 400 vintage whiskeys, including many pre-Prohibition bottles, that you can sample by the shot. As Callaway says, "You can taste bourbon history." The "Wabbit" is one of BBC's signature cocktails.

A boozy milk shake, the Entrepreneur, from Bottle & Bond Kitchen and Bar

Bottle & Bond Kitchen and Bar restaurant at Bardstown Bourbon Company

⌒∘ "Wabbit"

1 ounce Bardstown Bourbon Company Fusion Blend #1
¾ ounce carrot juice
½ ounce lemon juice
¼ ounce date syrup (see below)
3 drops Crude Bitters—Sycophant
Sage leaf for garnish

Combine all the cocktail ingredients in a shaker. Shake on ice and double-strain into a coupe glass. Garnish with a sage leaf.

DATE SYRUP
Macerate 1 pint of dates with rich syrup (1 pound of "sugar in the raw" and ½ pound of water, heated and stirred until the sugar dissolves).

*The "Wabbit" cocktail, Bottle &
Bond Kitchen and Bar*

Sweet potato gnocchi from Bottle &
Bond Kitchen and Bar

～ *Sweet Potato Gnocchi*

Serves 5

> 2 medium Idaho potatoes, baked, peeled, and riced
> 1 large sweet potato, baked, peeled, and riced
> 1 large egg
> ½ cup all-purpose flour
> 3½ tablespoons cornstarch
> Salt and pepper to taste
> Semolina flour to dust
> 2 ounces Parmesan, grated

Combine the riced potatoes and fold in the egg. Cool the mixture.

Mix the flour and cornstarch together in a bowl and season with salt and pepper. Add the dry mix to the potato mix. Incorporate just until a uniform consistency is achieved, as if you were making a pie dough. Knead just until smooth. Roll out the dough to long cylinders and cut into 1-inch pieces. Dust with semolina flour to keep from sticking.

Blanch the gnocchi and then sauté in butter until golden brown. Sprinkle with Parmesan.

Elmer T. Lee Clubhouse, Buffalo Trace Distillery, Frankfort

Buffalo Trace Distillery, Frankfort

https://www.buffalotracedistillery.com
800-654-8471 or 502-696-5926

Whiskey has been commercially distilled at the Buffalo Trace site since 1773, so the distillery's 400 acres are dotted with structures built by a succession of owners and in a variety of styles.

The casual, open-air Firehouse Sandwich Shop serves barbecue and sides from April through October. As the name suggests, it once served as the distillery's onsite fire station and was built in the 1930s.

The Elmer T. Lee Clubhouse (named for a former master distiller) dates from 1935. It was built with logs from Kentucky log cabins, some dating to the eighteenth century. Its inviting features are sure to attract guests in any season; there is a veranda with views of the beautifully landscaped grounds for warm weather and a wood-burning fireplace for wintertime. The Clubhouse is a venue for private events such as corporate meetings and weddings, as well as for special dinners hosted by the distillery.

Buffalo Trace's events manager Lucy Slusher notes, "We are especially proud of the Legendary Craftsmen Dinner Series." These multicourse dinners are created by nationally renowned chefs and paired with Buffalo Trace whiskeys. For example, one series brought chef Edward Lee (610 Magnolia, Milkwood, and Whiskey Dry restaurants in Louisville) to Buffalo Trace to match his dishes with George T. Stagg bourbon. Another featured a dinner by Paul Brantley, of Nashville's Southern Steak & Oyster, and E. H. Taylor whiskeys. A third paired William Larue Weller bourbons with creations from chef Giuseppe Tentori of GT Prime of Chicago. Lee created the following cocktail for the dinner he prepared at the distillery in 2019.

Whiskey Dry

½ ounce Buffalo Trace bourbon
1 ounce simple syrup
1 ounce apple cider
¾ ounce lemon juice
2 dashes Peychaud's bitters
Champagne

Shake all the ingredients (except the champagne) over ice and strain into a champagne flute. Top with champagne.

A statue of Colonel Albert Blanton, president of the distillery from 1921 to 1943, graces the lawn in front of the Elmer T. Lee Clubhouse, which he built. Blanton's wife, Bossy, had a famous recipe for puffed potatoes, which Lucy Slusher gave to us.

Bossy's Puffed Potatoes

2 cups mashed potatoes
2 tablespoons melted butter
2 well-beaten eggs
1 cup cream

Preheat the oven to 375 degrees. In a bowl, stir the melted butter into the mashed potatoes and beat until creamy. Add the eggs and the cream. Pour into a deep dish and bake until the potatoes are puffy and golden on top.

Table setting for Buffalo Trace dinner

Table setting for Buffalo Trace dinner

Wine and Spirits Guild dinner at Buffalo Trace

Maker's Mark Distillery, Loretto

https://www.makersmark.com/distillery
Star Hill Provisions, 270-685-7293

Chef Newman Miller oversees the kitchen at Star Hill Provisions, the onsite restaurant at picturesque Maker's Mark. Having spent some time at Chicago's award-winning North Pond restaurant, he brings sophisticated cooking techniques to traditional Kentucky fare. Miller loves to incorporate local ingredients into the dishes he creates, and many of the farmers who supply fresh produce are current or past distillery employees. Miller says, "We have a guy bringing us four different varieties of kale and I'm getting baby mustard greens. We get heirloom squash from a former dishwasher. We even get beef from a little farm in Oldham County."

Rob Samuels is the current president of Maker's Mark and the grandson of brand founders Bill and Margie Samuels. He is very conscious of his family's heritage of hospitality. "We try to entertain in the spirit of my grandmother," he says, "who set up the distillery in a very purposeful way, to make it feel much like welcoming visitors to our home." Samuels also sees the relative remoteness of Maker's Mark as an

Executive chef Newman Miller at Star Hill Provisions, Maker's Mark Distillery

Distillery grounds, Maker's Mark, Loretto

opportunity to invite visitors for an extended stay. "We are not right off I-65. People have to make an effort to get here, and we have an awful lot of visitors who, once they get to Maker's, don't want to leave. And we have a thousand acres we can use for visitor experiences." Part of that experience is the artwork commissioned by Samuels and incorporated into the distillery. These pieces include installations by internationally known blown-glass artist Dale Chihuly in the visitors' center lobby and in the ceiling of one of the warehouses.

Star Hill Provisions provides lunch (and cocktails) to day visitors. Distillery dinners are held on Saturday nights throughout the year. Miller and his staff also provide buffets for private events. The village-like collection of buildings and plantings by landscape designer Jon Carloftis creates the atmosphere of a festive garden party.

A long-standing entertaining tradition is the holiday open house, when the distillery is decorated with lights during the Christmas season. In addition to nighttime tours, it features music, a skating rink, and other family-friendly festivities.

Maker's Fancy Bourbon Punch

1 liter Maker's Mark bourbon
1 cup granulated sugar
Peels of 3 lemons and 1 orange
Juice of the peeled lemons and orange
1 liter strong, unsweetened tea (preferably green tea)
250 mL champagne (use club soda for a less fancy version)
Freshly grated nutmeg (or ground nutmeg if you don't have fresh)

Combine all the ingredients in a punch bowl and garnish with nutmeg. This is the perfect refreshing summer drink to serve to a crowd, especially in an outdoor setting. Ladle the punch into rocks glasses filled with ice.

Cold Smoked, Smothered Quail

Serves 2

4 whole, partially deboned quail
2 ounces smoked bacon, diced
1 red bell pepper, diced
1 white onion, diced
2 cloves garlic
2 tablespoons brown roux
2 cups reduced chicken stock
Salt and pepper
2 tablespoons Maker's Mark bourbon
2 tablespoons butter, cold
1 cup self-rising Weisenberger Mill cornmeal
Steamed and buttered rice or grits
Braised greens

Smoke the quail over used barrel bungs in a traditional grill with little to no heat. About 20 minutes of smoke is plenty for these little birds.

While the quails smoke, make the sauce. Cook the bacon over medium-low heat to render the fat and begin to crisp. When the bacon is almost cooked, add the red pepper, onion, and garlic and cook slowly until translucent. Add the roux followed by the chicken stock to create a nice-bodied sauce. Season with salt and pepper and let the sauce reduce slowly over low heat. When ready to serve, add the bourbon and butter to the sauce and stir well to combine.

When the quail is finished smoking, dredge in cornmeal and fry in clean oil set to 375 degrees until done, about 3 to 4 minutes. Place on a sheet pan to drain the excess oil.

Place 2 quail over each portion of rice and greens and cover with sauce.

Bourbon Women Sip-osium dinner at Maker's Mark Distillery

⌒ *Maker's Mark Sausage Balls*

Makes about 50 meatballs

2 sleeves saltine-style crackers, crushed
2 eggs
½ cup buttermilk
2 pounds good country sausage
1½ cups fresh shredded cheddar cheese

Preheat the oven to 450 degrees. In a large bowl, combine the crackers, eggs, and buttermilk and mix well. Add the sausage and cheese. Mix again, being careful not to overmix. Cover and let sit in the refrigerator for 30 minutes. Form the mixture into balls and place on greased baking sheets. Bake for 12 minutes and check. Bake for another 6 minutes or until cooked through. You want some browning and a crunchy exterior. Serve with Bourbon Mustard Dipping Sauce.

BOURBON MUSTARD DIPPING SAUCE
1 cup mayonnaise
3 ounces Marker's Mark bourbon
⅓ cup yellow mustard
2 tablespoons honey

Combine all the ingredients in a large bowl and mix well.

Maker's Mark sausage balls with Dijon mustard

Willett Distillery, Bardstown

https://www.kentuckybourbonwhiskey.com
502-348-0899

Founded by brothers Thompson and John Willett, the Willet Distillery opened in 1936, and it is still a family affair. Thompson's granddaughter Britt Kulsveen is the president of the company. Her brother, Drew Kulsveen, is the master distiller. Britt has a very clear notion of how visitors should be treated:

> Anyone who has ever visited our family's distillery most certainly leaves feeling—knowing, quite frankly—that they have visited our home, because it is our home. We are an independent family-owned and -operated business, and there is no distinction between family values that have been ingrained since . . . our birth and the values that we abide by, instill, and execute within our family business.

Willett Distillery president Britt Kulsveen

If I have my way, I will collect your cell phone at the door (I will have the kind decency to provide you with a coat-check ticket for your contraption), there will be no TV at the bar, and you will be forced to sip the most delicious whiskey cocktail barside or on the porch while you interact with that person sitting next to you. You may be served country ham and biscuits, chicken livers, and fried chicken, and you will like washing it all down with that mint julep made with Rowan's Creek [bourbon] and fresh mint plucked straight from our backyard.

Situated on wooded hills just outside of Bardstown, Willett Distillery is a little more informal than some of the others. Britt Kulsveen's footwear of choice—with any outfit from jeans to dresses—is cowgirl boots. The distillery has a beautiful bar upstairs in the visitors' center, where bartender Andy Pope creates cocktails using the full line of Willett whiskeys—both ryes and bourbons. The space now also features a restaurant. Tip: Try the catfish.

Here's a trio of favorite Willett cocktails:

Britt

1½ ounces Willett Family Estate 4-Year Rye
1 ounce house-made marasca syrup
2 dashes barrel-aged orange bitters
Champagne

Add the rye, marasca syrup, and bitters to a mixing beaker containing ice. Stir until chilled. Strain into a cocktail glass and gently pour a float of champagne on top.

⌒ Harvest Sour

1 ounce Willett Pot Still Bourbon
1 ounce applejack
¾ ounce lemon juice
¾ ounce simple syrup
Egg white
Dash of Angostura bitters for garnish

Add all the cocktail ingredients to a shaker and shake without ice (to emulsify the egg white); then add ice and shake vigorously. Garnish with a dash of Angostura bitters.

⌒ Blue Collar

The Blue Collar is a Manhattan variation originating in New York. It is a perfect after-dinner cocktail due to the digestif qualities of Amaro Ciociaro.

2 ounces Willett 4-Year Rye
½ ounce Cocchi di Torino
¼ ounce Maraschino
¼ ounce Amaro Ciociaro
2 dashes orange bitters
2 dashes Angostura bitters
Lemon twist for garnish

Add all the cocktail ingredients to a chilled mixing glass and add cracked ice. Stir for about 30 seconds. Strain into a chilled Manhattan glass. Garnish with a lemon twist.

OPPOSITE: *Harvest sour cocktail from Willett Distillery, Bardstown*

Woodford Reserve Distillery, Versailles

https://www.woodfordreserve.com
859-879-1812

The roads leading to Woodford Reserve Distillery wind through the iconic rolling green pastures where Thoroughbred horses graze and frolic, so visitors have the opportunity to experience both of Kentucky's signature industries. "For our dinner series, [guests] would do a tour of a horse farm, come back and tour the distillery, enjoy dinner. Then, having brought lawn chairs, they'd watch an outdoor movie about racing," says culinary and events manager Jenny Hurst. Movies for the series have included *Seabiscuit* and *Secretariat*. "We've also done Derby in June," Hurst says. For those outdoor dinners, guests wore their Derby finery—hats and colorful dresses and blazers—and partied at tables set beneath strings of fairy lights.

Woodford has long been committed to entertaining, and it was the first distillery to have a chef in residence: David Larson. Today's chef

Food and cocktail pairing at Woodford Reserve Best of Kentucky Dinner

in residence is Ouita Michel, owner of the Holly Hill Inn in nearby Midway. She helps plan menus and consults with chef de cuisine Charles Taylor.

The distillery's dryer house is the venue for indoor entertaining in the winter, which includes a long-standing series of holiday lunches in November and December. The visitors' center was expanded a few years ago and now includes a cocktail bar where visitors stopping by for a tour can enjoy Woodford's style of easy but elegant hospitality.

Dashing Double Oaked

1 ounce Woodford Reserve Double Oaked
½ ounce holiday spice syrup (see below)
Dash of Woodford Reserve Spiced Cherry Bitters
Rosemary for garnish

Combine the bourbon, syrup, and bitters in a rocks glass. Add ice, stir, and garnish with a sprig of rosemary.

HOLIDAY SPICE SYRUP
Place equal parts cloves, nutmeg, and aniseed in a clean, dry coffee grinder and grind to a fine powder. Put 1 liter of water in a deep pan and bring to a boil on high heat. Add 4¼ cups sugar and boil until you have a syrup of half-thread consistency. Strain the syrup through the spice mixture into another bowl.

Woodford Reserve Eclipse

1½ ounces Woodford Reserve Distiller's Select Bourbon
½ ounce Chambord
1 ounce cranberry juice
1 ounce raspberry juice
½ ounce lime juice
2 to 3 drops sorghum
Club soda, to top
Black raspberry and lime twist for garnish

Combine all the ingredients except the club soda and garnish in a shaker with ice. Shake vigorously, then strain into an iced glass. Top with a dash of club soda and garnish with a speared black raspberry and lime twist.

Entrée for Woodford Reserve Best of Kentucky Dinner

Al fresco Best of Kentucky Dinner at Woodford Reserve Distillery, Versailles

◠◠ Ouita Michel's Bourbon Beer Bread

Makes 1 loaf

    3 cups all-purpose flour, sifted
    1 tablespoon baking powder
    1 teaspoon iodized salt
    ¼ cup sugar
    1 12-ounce bottle Kentucky Bourbon Barrel Ale
    2 tablespoons Woodford Reserve bourbon
    ¼ cup (½ stick) melted butter

Preheat the oven to 375 degrees. Mix all the ingredients except the melted butter in a medium-size bowl. Pour into a greased loaf pan. Pour melted butter over the top and place in the middle of the preheated oven. Bake 45 minutes or until a toothpick inserted in the center comes out clean and the edges are golden brown. Remove from the pan and cool for at least 15 minutes.

◠◠ Woodford Reserve Chocolate Bread Pudding with Bourbon Butter Sauce

Serves 12 to 15

    12 cups stale French bread, diced in 1-inch cubes
    1 quart whole milk
    3 eggs, beaten
    1¾ cups sugar
    1 tablespoon vanilla
    1 teaspoon cinnamon
    6 ounces dark or bittersweet chocolate, chopped in large chunks
    3 tablespoons unsalted butter, melted

Place the bread cubes in a large bowl and toss with the milk until the bread is moistened. Soak for at least 1 hour.

Preheat the oven to 350 degrees. Whisk together the eggs, sugar, vanilla, and cinnamon and pour over the bread-milk mixture. Fold together until well mixed.

Fold in the chocolate chunks and mix until evenly distributed. Pour into a greased, deep 13- by 9-inch pan. Drizzle the melted butter over the batter and cover with foil.

Detail of table decorations at Woodford Reserve Best of Kentucky Dinner

Bake for 30 minutes covered and then for another 10 to 15 minutes uncovered, until the pudding is set and firm in the middle and golden brown on top. Serve warm with Bourbon Butter Sauce.

BOURBON BUTTER SAUCE

    8 ounces butter
    2 cups sugar
    ½ cup Woodford Reserve Distiller's Select Bourbon
    2 eggs

Melt the butter in a heavy-bottomed saucepan over medium heat. Whisk in the sugar and bourbon and bring to a simmer. Crack the eggs in a large bowl and whisk until blended. Add a little warm bourbon mixture to the eggs and whisk. Continue to add the bourbon mixture a little at a time until the eggs have been tempered. Pour all the liquid back into the pan and return it to medium heat. Bring to a light simmer and cook for several minutes, until thickened. Keep warm and serve over bread pudding.

ACKNOWLEDGMENTS

Many people helped us during the writing of this book. Thanks go to the very talented Kelly Crimi, Tabb Routt, and Margaret Horlander, whose efforts went above and beyond their normal jobs. Thanks to Utah Stevens, who helped style the photo shoots of table and bar settings. The photography was provided by Mac Brown, Chris Joyce, Jolea Brown, and the Bourbon Women Association.

Heather Wibbels, the Cocktail Contessa, generously supplied recipes for several of her creations for chapter 6. Thanks to the Kentucky Distillers' Association.

Photographs, comments, and recipes for chapter 8 were generously contributed by Garnett Black, Tracey Williamson, Dan Calloway, and Felix Mosso (Bardstown Bourbon Company); Lucy Slusher (Buffalo Trace); Rob Samuels, Newman Miller, and Dan Burgess of Doe-Anderson (Maker's Mark); Britt Kulsveen and Brittany Allison (Willett Distillery); and Chris Poynter, Jenny Hurst, Ouita Michel, and Charles Taylor (Woodford Reserve).

Thanks as well go to Linda Konner and Fred Minnick. And finally, a very big thank you to our families for their patient support during this project. Time to break out the family whiskey!

APPENDIX
Bourbon Resources

Ingredients and Party Sources

If you live outside of Kentucky, some ingredients such as grits, country ham, beaten biscuits, and Henry Bain's sauce may not be available. But don't despair. Authentic Kentucky foodstuffs are just a click of the mouse or a phone call away. And most of these places have retail stores that you can visit in person when you're in Kentucky; you can find the addresses on their websites.

Art Eatables

Makers of decadent chocolate truffles using a variety of Kentucky bourbons matched to the chocolate used in the candy.
https://arteatables.com
502-589-0210

Bourbon Barrel Foods

Incredible array of spices, condiments (including Henry Bain's sauce), and cocktail ingredients.
https://bourbonbarrelfoods.com
502-333-6103

Broadbent's Gourmet Market and Deli

Broadbent's has won the award for Grand Champion Country Ham at the Kentucky State Fair more times than any other producer. Whole hams and packaged slices are available.
https://www.broadbenthams.com
800-841-2202

Kentucky Gent

Premium cocktail mixes for bourbon-based drinks.
https://gentsgingerale.com
No phone number provided

Rebecca Ruth

The original bourbon ball candy maker. If you happen to be in Frankfort, take a tour of the factory, located in a modest frame house.
https://rebeccaruthonline.com
502-223-7475

Shuckman's Fish Co. & Smokery

In addition to spoonfish caviar, Shuckman's sells a variety of smoked fish (salmon, Kentucky rainbow trout, spoonfish) and seafood spreads. http://www.kysmokedfish.com/index.asp
502-775-6478

Taste of Kentucky

Everything from bourbon-infused barbecue sauces and jams to grits and beaten biscuits can be found here. This supplier carries foodstuffs from a variety of makers, most of which are members of Kentucky Proud, which certifies the authenticity of products of the state.
https://atasteofkentucky.com/
800-444-0552

Recommended Reading

We hope this book has gotten you excited about flavor pairings and bourbon cocktails. If you're eager for more information about bourbon, food, and cocktails, we have a few recommendations.

Fred Minnick's *Bourbon Curious: A Simple Tasting Guide for the Savvy Drinker*, 2nd ed. (Boston: Harvard Common Press, 2019) has an intriguing approach to bourbon appreciation. Fred categorizes bourbons as "grain-forward," "nutmeg-forward," "caramel-forward," and "cinnamon-forward." He also provides excellent accounts of bourbon history and how it is made today.

If your curiosity extends beyond bourbon to the rich history of cocktails, there is no better source than David Wondrich's *Imbibe! From Absinthe Cocktail to Whiskey Smash: A Salute in Stories and Drinks to "Professor" Jerry Thomas, Pioneer of the American Bar* (New York: Perigree Books, 2007).

The following titles would also be excellent additions to your bar and kitchen bookshelves.

Cocktail Books

All include history and lore as well as recipes.
Danger, Jane, and Alla Lapushchik. *The Bourbon Bartender: 50 Cocktails to Celebrate the American Spirit*. New York: Sterling Epicure, 2017.
Perrine, Joy, and Susan Reigler. *The Kentucky Bourbon Cocktail Book*. Lexington: University Press of Kentucky, 2009.
———. *More Kentucky Bourbon Cocktails*. Lexington: University Press of Kentucky, 2016.

Schmid, Albert W. A. *The Manhattan Cocktail: A Modern Guide to the Whiskey Classic.* Lexington: University Press of Kentucky, 2015.

———. *The Old Fashioned: An Essential Guide to the Original Whiskey Cocktail.* Lexington: University Press of Kentucky, 2013.

Wellman, Molly. *Handcrafted Cocktails: The Mixologist's Guide to Classic Drinks for Morning, Noon, and Night.* Cincinnati: Betterway Home Books, 2013.

Kentucky Cookbooks

Kentucky has a rich culinary history. This is only a small sample of cookbooks, but you'll find hundreds of recipes in them. The bibliographies in Albert Schmid's books will lead you to many more.

Benedict, Jennie. *The Blue Ribbon Cook Book.* 1922. Reprint, Lexington: University Press of Kentucky, 2008.

Hulsman, Lynn Marie. *Bourbon Desserts.* Lexington: University Press of Kentucky, 2014.

Jamie, Matt. *Eat Your Bourbon.* Louisville: Culinary Publishing, 2017.

Lundy, Ronni. *Shuck Beans, Stack Cakes, and Honest Fried Chicken.* New York: Atlantic Monthly Press, 1991.

Patteson, Charles, and Craig Emerson. *Charles Patteson's Kentucky Cooking.* New York: HarperCollins, 1988.

Schmid, Albert W. A. *Burgoo, Barbecue & Bourbon.* Lexington: University Press of Kentucky, 2017.

———. *The Kentucky Bourbon Cookbook.* Lexington: University Press of Kentucky, 2010.

From the Authors

For more advice on entertaining and curated entertaining pieces to use in your home, visit Peggy's website, www.peggynoestevens.com, and consult her book *Professional Presence: The Four-Part Guide to Building Your Personal Brand* (Phoenix: Greenleaf Book Group Press, 2012).

For descriptions of more than 400 bourbons, listed by distilleries and indexed by proof, price, and style, see Susan's book coauthored with Michael Veach: *The Bourbon Tasting Notebook,* 2nd ed. (Morley, MO: Acclaim Press, 2018).

GLOSSARY

The Bourbon Geek's Guide to Vocabulary

These definitions are excerpted from Susan's *Kentucky Bourbon Country: The Essential Travel Guide*.

angels' share: The liquid that evaporates from aging barrels (the proportion of whiskey and water depends on the barrel's location in the warehouse). Typically, about 10 percent of the total evaporates the first year and 3 to 4 percent each year thereafter.

barrel proof: Bourbon that is bottled directly from the barrel without adding water to adjust the proof. Because of evaporation during aging, the proof is typically high.

beading: The formation of bubbles when a bottle of bourbon is shaken. The larger the bubbles that form at the top, the higher the proof.

bonded bourbon (also **bottled in bond**): Originally, bourbon that was produced in a government-bonded warehouse for taxing purposes. Now it refers to a bourbon that is at least four years old and at least 100 proof. In addition, it must be the product of one distillery and one distiller in one season.

bourbon: American whiskey made from a fermented grain mash that is at least 51 percent corn. Its final distillation can be no higher than 160 proof, and it must be put in new (unused) charred oak containers (usually barrels) at no higher than 125 proof. There is no age requirement. As soon as the whiskey touches wood, it becomes bourbon. Note that very little bourbon made today is aged for less than four years. See also **straight bourbon**.

charring: The process in which the interior of a barrel is set on fire and allowed to burn for less than a minute. This cracks and blackens the wood, which allows the whiskey to penetrate the sides of the barrel.

chill haze: The cloudiness that appears at cool temperatures (such as when ice is added) if a bourbon is unfiltered or only lightly filtered.

congeners: The esters and fusel oils, mostly by-products of fermentation, that add flavor to bourbons. Tiny amounts are optimal; too much can produce off flavors.

corn whiskey: Whiskey made from 80 to 100 percent corn mash and aged in used or uncharred barrels.

esters: Aromatic organic compounds produced by yeast as a by-product of fermentation. They are responsible for many of the fruity, floral, and sweet spicy flavors in whiskey.

expressions: Different versions of a whiskey brand that vary by age or proof. For example, Old Forester comes in 86- and 100-proof expressions.

fusel oils: These alcohols, with a higher molecular weight than beverage alcohol, are present in tiny amounts in whiskey distillate. Higher amounts can produce off flavors.

heads and tails: The first and last distillates to come off the doubler, respectively. Since both contain impurities, they are returned to the still for further distillation. In some premium bourbons, the heads and tails are discarded rather than being distilled again.

malted barley (or simply **malt**): Partially sprouted barley that is roasted to stop germination. It is added to the mash bill to facilitate fermentation, since barley contains enzymes not found in corn, rye, or wheat. These enzymes help the yeast convert starch to fermentable sugars and then to alcohol.

mash bill: The recipe, or the proportion of each grain used to produce a particular whiskey.

master distiller: The bourbon maker assigned the overall responsibility for production and quality at a particular distillery.

mingling: The process of mixing bourbon from several barrels to create a consistent flavor profile. This is different from "blending," which is the process of adding flavors or aged spirits to grain-neutral spirits. By law, bourbons are never blended.

nose: The combination of aromas that can be detected by smelling bourbon in a glass. Equivalent to a wine's bouquet.

proof: Measure of the percentage of alcohol in a beverage, based on a 200-point scale. Thus, 90-proof bourbon is 45 percent alcohol by volume. The term (and the numbers) originated in the nineteenth century when buyers, seeking to verify that their whiskey had not been diluted, would mix it with gunpowder and light it. It would burn only if the whiskey was at least 50 percent alcohol, thus providing 100 percent "proof" that it was undiluted.

red layer: The layer of caramelized wood sugars formed when a barrel is toasted. This gives bourbon its color and much of its flavor.

rye whiskey: Whiskey made from a mash bill containing at least 51 percent rye.

single barrel: Whiskey bottled from a single barrel. The yield can range from 60 to 150 750-mL bottles, depending on how long the whiskey was aged and how much was lost to evaporation.

small batch: Whiskey bottled from the mingling of a small number of barrels. There is no prescribed number: some distilleries make small batches from as few as two barrels, and others may use a hundred or more.

small grains (or **smalls**): The grains other than corn, usually malted barley and rye or wheat, used to make bourbon and Tennessee whiskey.

straight bourbon: Bourbon that has been aged at least two years before bottling.

Tennessee whiskey: Whiskey that is almost identical to bourbon, with the same mash bill and aging requirements, but before it is put in the barrel, it is filtered through sugar maple charcoal. The two remaining distilleries that produce Tennessee whiskey are located in (surprise!) Tennessee: Jack Daniels (in Lynchburg) and George Dickel (in Cascade Hollow near Tullahoma).

toasting: Process of heating oak staves so they can be bent to make barrels. Produces the red layer.

wheated bourbon: Bourbon in which wheat has been substituted for rye in the mash bill.

yeast: Microscopic, single-celled fungi (*Saccharomyces cerevisiae*) that feed on the sugars present in mash. The by-products of their digestion are ethyl alcohol, carbon dioxide, heat, and a variety of fruity-smelling compounds (esters), depending on the yeast strain. Some distilleries, such as Brown-Forman, propagate their yeast onsite from frozen or liquid cultures. Others, including Buffalo Trace, add cakes of dry yeast directly to their fermenters.

RECIPE INDEX

GENERAL INDEX

presentation, 15–20, *16–19*, *21–22*; gifts, 25, *121*; invitations, 2, *4*; table and seating arrangements, *22*, 23, *24*

Peerless, 61

Perrine, Joy, 143

Pope, Andy, 179

presentation: appetizers, *16–19*, *110*; buffet, *21–22*; cocktails, *105*, *110*, *116*, *117*; decanters, *34–37*; food pairings, *67–68*, *70–71*, *72*, *73*, *85*; Kentucky Derby parties, 145, *145–51*; table settings, *23–24*; tastings, *50*, *53*, *59*

Rebel Yell, 49

Redbreast, 62

Redemption, 49

rye whiskey, 61

Sagamore Spirit, 61

Samuels, Rob, 172–73

Scotch whiskey, 61, 62

seafood, in pairings, 93

Seagram's VO, 62

seasonal themes, 14–15

seating and table arrangements, *22*, 23, *24*

side dishes, 80–82, 153–55, 167, 186

Slusher, Lucy, 167

snacks, *16–19*, 18, 44, 52, 75–76, 106–12, *108–10*, 176

Stagg Jr., 61

sugar cubes, *42*

table and seating arrangements, *22*, 23, *24*

Talisker, 62

tastings, 48–63; flights, 60–62, *63*; glassware, 51; mats, *51*, 51–52, *94*; presentation, *50*, *53*, *59*; steps, 55–57. *See also* cocktails

Tennessee whiskey, 61

Tentori, Giuseppe, 167

themes, 14–15, 31. *See also* Kentucky Derby parties

tourism. *See* distilleries

traditional bourbon, 49

Tullamore Dew, 62

vermouths, 120

Very Old Barton, 60

wheated bourbon, 49

whiskey: defined, 48; styles, 61–62

Whistle Pig, 62

Wibbels, Heather, 123

Wilde, Oscar, 45

Wild Turkey, 49, 61

Willet Distillery, 178–81

Willett, Thompson and John, 178

W. L. Weller, 49

Wondrich, David, 102, 106

Woodford Reserve: bourbon, 49, 69; distillery, 182–87

Wyoming Whiskey, 62

ABOUT THE AUTHORS

Bourbon Hall of Fame inductee Peggy Noe Stevens is a trailblazer for women. She is the world's first female master bourbon taster and the founder of the Bourbon Women Association. She was also one of the originators of the iconic Kentucky Bourbon Trail. She received the prestigious Networking Award from the Kentucky Distillers' Association. Stevens is a certified etiquette, image, and professional speaker and is the author of *Professional Presence: A Four-Part Guide to Building Your Personal Brand* and *The Culinary Cocktail Tour.* She is a contributing writer for *American Whiskey Magazine* and entertaining editor for *Bourbon+.*

Among award-winning writer Susan Reigler's books are *Kentucky Bourbon Country: The Essential Travel Guide, The Kentucky Bourbon Cocktail Book,* and *The Bourbon Tasting Notebook.* From 1992 to 2007, Reigler was restaurant critic and beverage columnist for the *Louisville Courier-Journal.* Currently she is a contributing writer for *Bourbon+, American Whiskey Magazine,* and *LEO Weekly* and bourbon columnist for *Food & Dining.* Reigler is past president of the Bourbon Women Association and has been featured at whiskey festivals throughout the United States, including in Chicago, New Orleans, and Louisville. She is a certified executive bourbon steward and a graduate of Indiana and Oxford Universities.